C000075706

Cricut Projects

~

63 Awesome and Inspiring Projects

Written By Angela Carson

ISBN: 9781091006850

Table of Contents

Introduction

After the publishing of my previous book 'cricut projects for beginners' people asked me to publish another book about cricut projects. I listened and created this follow-up book with a lot more projects.

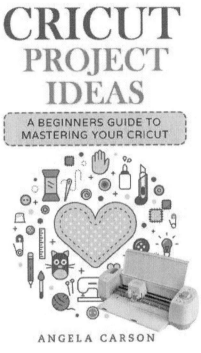

My previous book

Throughout this book, you will find a variety of different cricut projects. Some will be easy, and some will be more challenging. The selection is to get your creativity flowing and your mind reeling from all the different things your Cricut can do.

This book assumes you already know the basics. If you are a beginner, read the manual provided for your machine on the cricut website. You will be up and running in no-time.

There are a few chapters toward the end of the book to offer you guidance on different materials, accessories, and techniques for successful crafting.

Before you begin, take a moment to think about the next few months. Do you have a few birthdays coming up or an anniversary? What about a holiday or party you are hosting? Did you get invited to a dinner party or event and do not know what to bring the host?

You do not have to keep giving the same, old generic gift over and over again because it is "easy." You own a Cricut! Now you can give something personal, meaningful, handmade, and awesome! Use the projects in this book to get you going and leap into the amazing, world of DIY cricut projects.

Yes, it is great to give others a wonderful gift you made just for them, but think about yourself a little bit, too. Is there a fun t-shirt you always wanted or a piece of artwork you know would look great over your fireplace but just have never "splurged" on it?

You can elevate your wardrobe and your home for a little part of what it would cost you retail. Etch glass cups, make metal coasters, design bags and shirts, make creative art, and so much more. You can do it all! The "world is your oyster!"

I hope you enjoy this book like I have enjoyed making it!

Professionally Designed Cards

Thank You Card

Project inspired by Joann Fabrics

When you want to thank someone with a special, personal card, there is no better way than with this great design.

You'll need:
- Cardstock in cream and tan
- Cricut Pen – this will enable you to write professionally on the card.

Step 1
Open Design Space and choose your thank you card design. If you want to choose a pre-designed option, you will have plenty to choose from, but you can also develop your own with your own message and image.

Step 2

Once you load your design, you will want to load your cardstock into your Cricut machine on the cutting pad and print and cut your design.

If you decide that you want to have the machine write a personal message in the card for you, you can "activate" this feature. It is a great feature because you can write and cut at the same time. In addition, this is what makes the image appear to be three-dimensional like the example above.

Additionally, this helps relieve the stress of creating a custom card by doing the writing and cutting for you.

Step 3

If you are creating a design similar to the one in the example image, you will want to load your second color of cardstock on your mat to be cut. You do not need to know when to do this, just follow the prompts in Design Space on your computer. When all the pieces are cut and printed, all you have to do is slide them together or attach them with a few dots of glue or double-stick tape.

Custom Envelope Liners

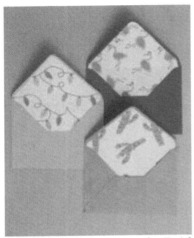

Project thanks to Bespoke Bride

Any special occasion deserves special attention, including to your envelopes. You can use all sorts of different prints or images to grace the inside of your envelopes, like personal photographs or corresponding prints. The wonderful thing about adding this to your envelope means the people getting your message can get a hint about your message before they even read a word!

If you print an image from your computer, make sure to print it on high-quality photo paper for the best results. In this specific project, the envelope is designed to house a 5"x7" card.

You'll need:
- An image or print you want
- Various colorful paper envelopes designed for 5"x7" cards
- Double stick tape

Step 1
Begin by choosing a high-quality image for your envelope. It can be a good quality JPEG image or even a nice photograph! Remember, you will be cropping off the top of the image to fit the top of the envelope flap so if you choose a photograph, make sure there is space on the sides to allow for this cropping. Also, make sure your image is a minimum of seven inches wide to fit the inside of the 5" x 7" envelope.

Step 2
Search for the "envelope liner" template in Design Space. When prompted, choose the "simple image" option. You can maintain the backdrop they suggest or delete it if you want. Once you are done, choose "Save as a Cut Image."

Step 3
On this screen, upload the image you have chosen. Make sure your corners of the image align with the corners of the envelope. The size of the envelope in the example is seven inches, so make sure your image is adjusted to this now if it was not already. Now insert a score line on the image where the fold of the flap is so the envelope will fold properly.

Step 4
Send your file to cut. In some cases, you may have decided to print the file on your computer printer and then load it into your Cricut to just cut and score. Other times, you may want to print the file from your Cricut and have it on the mat, too. It just depends on your image and preference! If you have your Cricut print it, keep in mind there is a limited capability for printing photographic-quality images.

Step 5
Once your image is printed and cut, remove it from your mat and use the scoreline to fold your liner. It is best to use the scraper tool to make sure the fold line is well creased.

Step 6
Carefully apply strips of the double-stick tape to the backside of the image and begin inserting the liner into the inside of the envelope. Focus on adding strips of tape to the edges of the flap.

Step 7
Once you insert the liner into the envelope, use your scraper tool to go over the edges and press it securely down into the envelope. This makes sure that the image is secure and no bubbles remain.

Step 8
Now that your envelope is lined, add your personal note inside, seal it up, and send it off! You will definitely impress your recipients with your thought and creativity!

Ice Cream Greeting Card

Project thanks to Inspiration Made Simple

When you need to make a quick, sweet card for someone special, this is a great go-to project. It is simple and pre-loaded in Design Space. All you have to do is click on "Make It." Create several in different colors with complimentary envelopes to be able to grab when the need arises.

You can also adjust the message on the front if you want something a little different or leave the pen off, so you do not have any drawings on the card. You can always add your own drawings to it later if you want.

You'll need:
- Polka dot, tan, red, pink, and cream cardstock
- Standard grip mat
- Foam adhesive dots
- Scoring stylus
- Glue, preferably a glue stick
- Black pen
- Double-stick tape and spray adhesive, optional

Step 1
Follow the instructions on design space to place the corresponding cardstock on the mat. Place the mat into the machine and follow the prompts.

Step 2
When the instructions call for it, load the stylus and then the pen into the machine.

Step 3
Once all the parts are cut out and designed, you can begin to assemble. Begin by folding the cream, exterior part of the card in half and mark gently with a pencil where to place the pink ice cream piece. Use the glue stick to attach the ice cream top on the inside of the card. If you want a more 3-d look, consider attaching the ice cream top with foam adhesive dots.

Step 4
On the front of the card, attach the tan ice cream cone. Use the spray adhesive for best results if you have it or the glue stick. Situate it below the cut out of the ice cream scoop and next to the words on the front.

Step 5
Use a foam adhesive dot to attach the red strawberry on top of the ice cream.

Step 6
Assemble the envelope by folding along the scoring lines. Use the glue stick or double-stick tape to secure the edges.

Step 7
If you want to line the inside of the envelope with another piece of cardstock, consider cutting another envelope template and trim the edges of the card by ¼ inch. Using the spray adhesive, glue the two envelopes together with the printed side facing out. Fold along the score lines and secure with the glue stick or double-stick tape. Double-stick tape will be best if you have it.

Spinning Heart Card

Project inspired by Crafting in the Rain

Spinner cards offer a variety of fun messages that you can send. The example is "love" theme with a glittering heart, but you can change the message, colors, and spinning shape to be anything you want. Think of spinning images like boats, people, airplanes, flowers, etc. There is no limit to what you can do with this template!

You'll need:
- Two pennies
- Foam dots or circles
- Glue
- Pink and white cardstock
- Grey faux-leather cardstock or material
- Blue craft foam

Step 1
Open the Spinner Card design file in Design Space. Cut the cardstock as instructed, following the prompts.

Step 2
Using glue, add the grey, faux-leather cardstock to the pink card base, aligning it in the center of the front side of the card.

Step 3

Add the foam to the back of the white cut cardstock. On the front of the white part, add words or images that align with the theme of your card. Do not put anything that pops out from the card close to the cut put track as it will interfere with your spinning object later on.

Step 4

Lay one penny on the table and then place the white cardstock on top with the blue foam facing down to the table, lining up the middle of the penny in the visible track. Glue the small blue foam circle on the penny in the middle of the track, being careful not to get any glue on the edges of the track. Carefully glue the second penny on top of the first that now has the foam dot attached. Allow to dry completely before moving.

Step 5

Glue the white circle of cardstock on the top of the penny that is on the design side of your white cardstock front, not on the side with the blue foam. Glue your spinning image on top of the white circle. Allow to dry completely before moving again.

Step 6

Once your glue is dry and your spinning image is secure, glue the white part to the pink and grey card base, aligning the white in the center of the grey faux-leather background. Allow to dry completely and then test your spinner!

Flower Partner Cards

Project inspired by Going Buggy

This card is a little bit of Cricut, a little bit of painting, and a whole lot of fun! Plus, it makes two cards in one tutorial, so you get two for the effort of one. Mix up the design and choose a cut out other than a flower to make it a more customized design. You can also adjust the colors and messaging to fit any occasion.

You'll need:
- Variety of alcohol inks, such as coral and bronze
- White cardstock
- Spray adhesive
- Stamp with a favorite saying and ink
- White embossing supplies or adhesive words in white
- White 6x6 card base, quantity: 2
- Prima flower, large
- Brass brad or two-pronged fastener
- Added sentiment sticker or quote, quantity: 2
- Embossed floral cardstock
- Liquid pearls or silver puffy paint

Step 1
Search Design Space for a droopy headed flower shape. The Cindy Lou cartridge offers a variety of flower options that work well for the project. Cut the image 5 inches on the white adhesive vinyl or cardstock, depending on what you have chosen to use.

Step 2
Using your stamp, add the words all over the front of the white card base. If you choose, you can print a quote or saying on the card base if you prefer instead of hand stamping it.

Step 3

Attach the flower cut out to the card in the place you want it to appear. Use the spray adhesive to make sure the image stays in one place.

Step 4

Using the alcohol inks, dab with a sponge applicator liberally all over the front of the card, covering and combining colors. Before the paints dry completely, while still tacky, peel off the flower cut out, revealing the stamped white base underneath. If the page appears too white for you, dab some distressed ink on top, such as the linen distress.

Step 5

Use the same colors and sponge applicator to add color to the Prima flower petals. Fold the flower in half and press it onto the card base over the head of the removed flower image. Use the brass brad to secure in place. If you prefer, consider using a foam or glue dot to secure the flower to the top of the image instead of the brad.

Step 6

On the other card base, emboss or adhere words in white over the entire front part of the card.

Step 7

Cut a piece of the embossed cardstock about 5 inches tall and 2 inches wide. Scallop one side of the strip. Dab bronze ink over the piece and adhere it to the front of the card with glue dots or foam adhesive dots.

Step 8

Use glue dots or foam adhesive dots to attach the cardstock flower peeled from the first card to the front of the new card base. Also, attach a new sentiment sticker or label to the bottom corner of the card.

Step 9
Add small dots with liquid pearls or "puffy paint" to the flower for more dimension and interest. You can do silver as pictured or a less-contrasting color like bronze or coral if you prefer.

Burlap Greeting Card

Project inspired by 100 Directions

A simple, rustic-looking card can give a unique touch to a nice sentiment.

You'll need:
- Pink foil iron on vinyl
- White iron on vinyl
- 6x6 white card base
- Burlap
- Crafting glue

Step 1

Design your images and words in Design Space. You can create something new or adapt a preset template. Send your images to be cut, including the words and a heart in pink foil, the base, scrolling image in white, and the burlap rectangle. The burlap should measure about 5.5"x5.5".

Step 2

When the vinyl is printed, use your weeding tool to remove the unnecessary pieces.

Step 3

Attach the vinyl to the burlap. This is not an easy process because of the rough weave of the burlap. Warm your iron to 325 degrees and press the vinyl to the burlap for 30 seconds. Do this process at least three times to help it adhere securely to the burlap. Allow to cool before peeling off. It will not be a smooth transfer, but the lumps and wrinkles add to its shabby-chic appearance.

Step 4

Using the glue, attach the burlap to the middle of the card base. If the edges of the burlap are fraying too much, dab a little glue around the sides to keep the burlap intact.

Thank-a-teacher Card

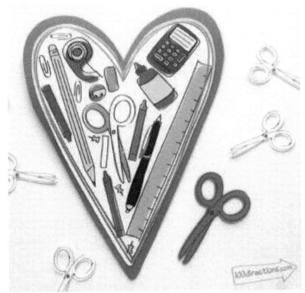

Project inspired by 100 Directions

Show your appreciation for the teachers in your life with this fun little card and matching scissor confetti. Add the confetti to the inside of the card or a present.

You'll need:
- Pink, teal, and white cardstock
- Spray adhesive or glue dots
- Heart and Scissor and School Supplies Heart template by Jen Goode in Design Space

Step 1
In Design Space, find the Teacher Card make-it-now canvas and follow the prompts to mark and cut the file.

Step 2
After completing the print and cut, use your weeding tool to remove the excess pieces.

Step 3
Using your adhesive, attach the front printed heart to the teal heart card base. Then attach your message heart to the inside of the card. You can glue some of the scissor confetti pieces to the inside of the card if you want.

Step 4
Add loose scissor cutouts inside the card as confetti or put inside a gift that accompanies the card. This cut file does not come with an envelope so make your own with a simple cardstock fold or use the photo-lined envelope template shown earlier in this chapter!

Happy Father's Day Card

Project inspired by A Little Craft in Your Day

This is an excellent, foundational tutorial for any card base with basic writing. Change it up from Father's Day to any other message and design you want to send. Also, consider printing on colored paper to match a present or theme, if you want.

You'll need:
- White cardstock
- Scoring stylus
- Silver and black pens

Step 1
Begin with opening Design Space and uploading your chosen image to a blank canvas. Choose any image or images from the library. In this example, the words, "Happy Father's Day" and a blue and white striped tie were used. Do not look for just black and white images to complete this project. You will be removing color in the next few steps.

Step 2
To create the card base, create a "square" shape and adjust it to your card size. In this example, it is 4" x 8". Drag the square to adjust to your desired size. Make sure to also add your score line halfway through the card. You can find this under "shapes" as well. To make sure it is placed properly, select the scoreline and the card shape and, in the upper toolbar, select "align" and then "centers."

Step 3
Adjust your images to fit inside your card front and drag images to place them where you want to print them. Select the images and then click on "write" on the right-side toolbar. This is what will remove the interior coloring.

Step 4
Select the word image and change the color to "black," and then select the tie and then change the color to "silver."

Step 5
Select all the layers and click on "Attach" and then "Make It." Follow the prompts for scoring, writing, and medium cardstock.

Paper Cut Birthday Card

Project inspired by Paper Mill Direct

Another great basic card design is a paper cut design. This tutorial is a basic outline that can be applied to a variety of images and messages. Customize according to whom you are planning on giving the card to or time of the year. Think of something like "Happy Holidays" and a pine tree or wreath for Christmas or "We're Going to Disney!" and a Disney character like Mickey Mouse. The options are endless.

You'll need:
* White and navy cardstock
* Glue or spray adhesive

Step 1
In Design Space, create a square and adjust the size to 5" x 7".

Step 2
Next, upload the image you want to use. In this example, it is a motorcycle. When the image is on the canvas, separate the layers and delete the ones you do not want to use. This should leave you with an outline of the image you want.

Step 3
Duplicate the rectangle you created and scale it down slightly to fit inside the first rectangle. Consider sizing it 3" x 5". Slide the smaller rectangle on the top of the larger one and then select both rectangles. Select "Align" and then "Center Vertically" and then "Center Horizontally."

Step 4
To remove the unnecessary rectangles, highlight both the rectangles and then select "slice." This allows you to delete the overlapping center rectangles you do not want. This creates a frame for your image and words.

Step 5
Drag your motorcycle image into the frame. Make sure the image touches on the right and left sides of the frame. When you are satisfied with the placement, select "weld" to create a single piece.

Step 6
To add text to your images, select "text" and write the message you want, such as "Happy Birthday" and "Kevin." The font used is "Stencil" because it is best for cutting. It does not leave any remaining pieces in the process. You can play around with whatever font you want but keep that in mind.

Step 7
When you have your message written and adjusted, select the first group of words and align horizontally so it is perfectly centered along the top and then do the same for the bottom.

Step 8

Add another rectangle, this one measuring 5.5" x 7.5" and place it behind the designed frame. Recolor it to blue to tell the machine that you want to cut a new piece from a different cardstock.

Step 9

When you are ready, select "Make it" and follow the prompts for medium cardstock.

Step 10

When the pieces are cut, weed out any remaining parts that you do not want. Attach the background color to the front image and message. Write your personal message on the back if you want. You can also create this as a folded card by creating the back colorful rectangle as 11" x 15" and adding a score line in the center.

Other Paper Crafts

Coloring Pages

Project inspired by 100 Directions

Kids and adults alike enjoy spending time coloring images. Both age groups find it relaxing and adults especially benefit from the stress reduction the activity offers. Instead of spending a lot of money on books and store-bought pages, try creating your own! It is easy and quick with just about any theme.

You'll need:
- Paper or cardstock
- Cricut Pen – for any customized writing
- Standard grip cutting mat

Step 1

On your workspace in Design Space, insert the image that you want as your coloring page. Popular images are mandalas or general black and white images for kids. Make sure you choose or adjust the chosen image to fit the size of the page you want to create. If you are not sure how big to make it, consider starting with the size of your paper or cardstock and then adjust to your preference on your second design.

Step 2

Sometimes you may want to layer images and add more than one to your design. If you do this, just make sure you add and adjust this image accordingly as well.

Step 3

Select the image and choose "Ungroup." This breaks the layers of the image apart that you can select and delete. Remove all the layers with color and anything else you do not want printed. When you are done, select "Regroup" to bring the image back together. If you have more than one image on your workspace, you will want to do this to each image.

Step 4

Make sure you are satisfied with the results of your editing. Once you are ready, you are going to send it to print. While it is printing, your image on your chosen paper or cardstock will also trim your coloring page you set your workspace to create.

Gift Tags

Project inspired by This Heart of Mine

This project is like making a greeting or thank you card outlined in the first chapter, but a more simplified process. It can pretty much be any design you can think of, but it does need to be a flat image.

You'll need:
- Cardstock
- Selection of Cricut pens, if desired

Step 1
Open Design Space and import the images you want to use on your gift tags. This could include the shape of the tags, words, and colors of the tags.

Step 2
Once you lay out your gift tag designs, add a small circle to the top to be cut out. This is where you will pass string or ribbon through the tag. Once this last feature is added, send the file to cut by clicking on "Make It."

If you are interested in multi-dimensional tags, create layers with additional text or images that will be attached or strung together. Cricut will alert you when you need to add new paper to a cutting mat and how it should be relatively easy to assemble.

Step 3
Once the file is cut, remove from your cutting mat and assemble your pieces. If there are any small pieces that are still stuck to your designs, like the small circle for your string or ribbon, use your weeding tool to remove the unwanted pieces. This is usually best done while still on the mat.

To add more decoration to your tags, consider adding a bit of glitter to the tags or extra little pieces, such as a small tree, star, or snowflake cut out.

Cupcake Wrappers

Project inspired by Wholeport

Are you planning a themed party, must make goodies for an upcoming event, or want to do something special with your family? Then this is the project for you! It creates a great visual and message for the family, friends, and guests.

You'll need:
- Paper or cardstock—that's it!

Step 1
Open Design Space and search the library for cupcake liners or wrappers. There is a selection on the website, or you can develop your own. Set the canvas to the size of your cardstock or paper and make as many wrappers as you can. You do not need to make a minimal number of wrappers because you can always use them again in the future! Keep in mind that a standard cupcake needs a wrapper that is about nine inches long.

Step 2

When you have your design set, place your paper or cardstock on the mat and send the file to cut. Follow the prompts on your computer and your machine to finish cutting the designs.

Step 3

Use your weeding tool to remove any small pieces that did not come out while cutting. If your design did not call for it, add a small cut on the top on one side and the bottom on the other. This cut should extend about halfway up the wrapper. If you used a pre-set cupcake wrapper, it probably already included it. This means when you wrap your cupcake with the wrapper, you will slide the top into the bottom to close the wrapper.

If you do not want to make a slice in your design, use a few glue dots to glue the design together instead.

Top Tip: If you are designing wrappers for a child's event, cut out your wrappers and then give the paper to your kids to color and design before you put them around the treats. It adds a great, personal touch!

A Bookmark

Project inspired by UK Cricut

It may seem a little archaic to have or give a custom bookmark, but it is still practical and very personal. Plus, it is a simple project you can do fast!

You'll need:
- Vinyl
- Paper of cardstock

Step 1
Bookmarks can be just about any size and shape you desire, so when you open Design Space, create a shape you prefer. In this example, the bookmark is about two inches wide and six inches tall. These include text that is cut out from the bookmark, so choose any word or phrase you want to appear and adjust the size and font to your liking. You can always add a picture or other details if you want.

Step 2

To cut the vinyl out of the vinyl of the bookmark, make sure to select your text and tell the software to set the text as a separate layer and then select "Attach."

Step 3

Send the file to cut and follow the prompts on your screen. Once the bookmarks are cut and assembled, if you have a laminator, consider laminating them to help them last even longer and bring an even more professional appearance to your project.

Napkin Holders

Project thanks to Laura's Little Party

Make your next dinner party standout with personal and custom napkin holders. You can make them in any design you like to match your dinner party theme or season.

You can also make it as simple as possible, with just a few images or words, or more complicated with multiple materials and pieces.

Choose a version based on your comfort and preference level. In addition, you can also decide how you want to attach your holders.

For example, you can add small slits on the top on one end of the holder and one on the bottom of the other to slide into each other, or you can use a glue dot. You can even use a small strip of double-stick tape to enclose the holder. You could also add small holes on either side of the holder and lace ribbon or string through it.

You'll need:
- Colored or glitter cardstock
- Vinyl, if preferred
- Your closure method of choice: glue dots, double-stick tape, etc.

Step 1
In Design Space, design the text or names that you want to appear on your napkin wraps. Make sure it is adjusted so the words will appear appropriately on your wrap width. This is also the time to develop a layer with the flourishing details, like the olive branch, and the shape of your napkin wrap. Also, think about images and different shapes you could include on your napkin holders.

Step 2
With your napkin wrap base designed, repeat your patterns and words on the number you need for your place settings. This is what will tell your Cricut to cut multiple pieces and allows you the opportunity to customize each one if you desire.

If you are going to be closing the wraps with ribbon and need holes or want to slide the ends together with slits, make sure to add those in now.

Step 3

Once you have your designs laid out, send the file to cut. Weed out any small items you do not want in your design. Assemble your napkin wrap pieces and wrap your napkins or silverware for your big event! Make sure to attach them securely according to the method you have chosen.

Magnetic Paper Flowers

Project thanks to My Sparkled Life

Adding a few bright flowers to your fridge can take your kitchen from average to extraordinary. It can help it go from a place you "have" to be to a place you "want" to be! You can create as many as you want, in any color or pattern that matches your décor.

You can also come up with a variety of flowers to suit your mood or help you keep track of your family needs. They are also awesome gifts!

You'll need:
- Cardstock in a variety of colors or patterns
- Hot glue gun
- Magnets

Step 1

Open Design Space and develop the shape of your petals. These look good as half circles or oval shapes. You can also create bumped petal shapes by stacking oval over one another. Repeat the petal shapes to make enough flower magnets that you want. A large flower typically has about 12 petals while a medium one has about eight.

Medium petals are about two inches long while large petals are usually about three inches. Measure the size of your magnet base and develop a circular flower base. If you want to, you can add a small, ½ inch long slit at the end of every petal for easiest construction.

Step 2

Once you have your petals designed and duplicated, load the cardstock on your cutting mat and get it ready to cut. Send the file to cut. If you did not add the slit in Design Space, use a crafting knife or an Exacto knife to cut a slit at the bottom of each petal.

Once all the petals have a cut, add a dot of glue and glue one side to the other making them into the petal shape. Do this to all the petals.

Step 3

Place your magnets down on the table and gather all the base circles and glue them to the tops of the magnets. Begin gluing the petals to the circle bases, starting on the outside and working your way in.

Continue adding petals until it looks full. Large flowers will have about three or more layers, while medium may only have two. Keep playing with your petals until you have a shape and set up that looks best to you. Leave a small space in the center of the flower open.

Step 4
Go back to Design Space and create smaller petals. Make them slightly smaller than the first petals. These are designed to add to the center of your flowers, so adjust them according to what you want. If you are unsure, try a few different shapes to try them out.

Add the slits to the petals again or wait until after they are cut to add the slits with an Exacto knife. When you are ready, send the file to cut. Create the petal shapes with a little bit of glue.

Step 5
Add glue to the interior of the flower design and begin adding the smaller petals to the inside of your flowers. Gently pinch the edges of your flowers for a more geometric appearance or gently curve them inside for something more natural. You can add as many petal layers as you like.

Art Journals

Project inspired by Kim Dellow

These sweet little notebooks are great for art and travel journals, but you can really customize them to fit any need or desire. Choose favorite colors and patterns, personalized sayings or words, and you can even add a few more pages to the inside if you want. Get ready for some serious jealous looks the next time you pull one of these out of your bag!

You'll need:
- Glue
- Colored thread
- Large needle
- Paper piercer or something to poke holes in your paper
- Various cardstock in interesting prints
- Various paper in interesting colors and prints

Step 1

In Design Space, create a square on your canvas. Round the corners. You may want to ungroup the layers and delete the bottom layer. Also, adjust the size of your square to the size of your final notebook. For example, in this example, the notebooks are 5" x 7". This means your square will need to measure 10" x 7".

Step 2

Add your scoreline to the middle of the square or rectangle shape. You will find this line under "lines." Adjust the size to fit your project and then select "Align" and "Center." This should automatically adjust the line so it is directly in the middle of your project.

Step 3

Next, add notches to your center score line to tell you where to pierce your paper. You can place another score line at 90 degrees from the centerline and scale it down so it is small. Alternatively, you can place a very small circle over the place you want to pierce your paper and have the machine cut the little spot out for you. Measure down about one inch from the top and bottom to place your holes or notches.

Step 4

If you want to add any custom cut outs or stickers to the front cover, you can now design those as you desire. Otherwise, you can use shapes and stickers you already have on hand. You can always create these later as well.

Step 5

Now you are ready to create the inside pages of your book. You will want to copy and paste the cover rectangle piece and make the pages just slightly smaller than the cover. Consider the size 9.8" x 6.8".

This means you will also want to re-align your center score line. You will also need to adjust the size. Do not move your notch or hole marks, though! Keep those one inch from the top and bottom of the cover, not the page!

Step 6
If you moved the notches or hole marks, you can always group the markings from the cover and copy and paste them for as many pages of the book you are creating. Then move, do not resize, these markings and place them over the centerline of each page.

Step 7
If you want to add images and cut outs to the internal pages, you can add those now. Keep in mind that any words you cut out on one side of the page will appear back on the other side! Consider using images and shapes to be safe. You can also create vinyl stickers or drawn images to the pages if you do not want to cut into the paper. If you choose vinyl words or images, some art mediums may struggle to cover them properly.

Step 8
When you are done designing your pages, send your file to print, cut, and score your cover and pages. Follow the prompts to load your paper and tools into your machine.

Step 9
After your pages and cover are cut, fold on the score line and place the pages into the cover and line up the notches or holes. If you are using notches, use your paper punch to poke holes in the cover and paper where the notches are located. Depending on your paper, you may want to punch holes one at a time.

Step 10
Thread your needle with the colored thread. Pass your needle through the holes and tie a slip knot. Tighten your knot as tight as possible and then tie off with a regular knot. You can tie on the outside of the journal or on the inside. Trim the threads as short as you want.

Step 11
If you are decorating your cover, make sure you add stickers or vinyl to the cover as you prefer. Now you are ready to start journaling away!

Paper Succulents in a Container

Project inspired by The Happy Scraps

This pretty little project can be made to fit into any container you already have and can instantly add a little punch to your mantelpiece, table setting, or display. Make as many or as few of these different succulents as you want.

You'll need:
- Cardstock in teals and pinks
- Ink pads in different coordinating colors of teal and pink
- Sponges or dabbers for the ink
- Hot glue gun
- Foam to fill your container

Step 1

In Design Space, look for the design file for succulents. If you want to create the design yourself, create one large petal shaped flower and then copy it about six times. Scale each copy down to a smaller size.

If you need to, remove a petal or two to make it appear more proportional. For the spiral and pointed succulent, make a spiral with three rings. The center of the ring should be a circle on the end. Add pointed triangles to the outside of the spiral lines.

Step 2

Once you have your designs ready, send your file to cut on your different colored card stock. Remove your pieces and place corresponding flower pieces together on a covered work surface. Using your sponges or dabbers, add a touch of ink to the outer edges of each petal shape or on the tips of the spikes of the spiral. You can keep the colors matching or contrast with a pink tip on a teal succulent and vice versa.

Step 3

Gently curl the edges of the petals up on the ends to make them more three-dimensional.

Step 4

Using your hot glue gun, glue the layers of the succulents together and roll the pointed succulents and glue them together as well.

Step 5

Place the floral foam inside your container, about ½ inch from the top. You can place your succulents on the foam or glue them down in the place where you like the arrangement.

Once all your succulents are placed, consider covering the exposed foam with paper grass or shredded paper. You can glue this covering down if you like but it typically looks best when it is loose.

Giant Paper Flowers

Project inspired by Jennifer Maker

Glam up a nursery wall, a hallway, a party, wedding, or any other notable event or space with these amazing flowers! Get creative with the colors or even try out patterned paper for a totally different effect.

You'll need:
- A marker for rolling petals
- Hot glue gun
- Pink cardstock, at least 17 pages
- Flower file from Design Space library

Step 1

Open the flower file in Design Space. It will make a 3-inch circular base, 2 petals for the interior rosebud, 6 4-inch smaller petals, 8 5.5-inch medium petals, 8 7-inch large petals, and 8 8-inch extra-large petals. The file will appear that all the petals are overlapping — it is ok and will cut properly once you hit "Make It." Be prepared to send your file to cut and use all 17 sheets of paper. If you are not using a file from the Cricut library, use the dimensions described above to make your own petal shapes.

Step 2

Once all the petals are cut out, glue the bottoms of the petals together with your hot glue gun so it creates a cupped shape to the petal. It is best to do a single line of glue on one side of the slit in the petal base and then overlaps the other side and press gently. This is for all the extra-large, large, medium, and small petals.

Step 3

To shape the outer edge of each petal, use the marker and roll the petal outwards. You can curl only the top of the petals, but you can also experiment with rolling the sides as well. In addition, make sure to roll the petals out, not in. It will look better when finished.

Step 4

Create the interior rosebud now. Apply glue to one edge of a petal and roll it inside and attach it to another petal. Roll that petal and glue it to the edge of the first petal.

Leave about ½-inch in the center, about the size of your pointer finger. Take the other petals and wrap them around the first, gluing them in place, but with about another ½-inch in between the petals.

Step 5
Add the small petals to the rosebud. Glue them around the rosebud trying to keep that ½-inch distance between each petal for best results. Set the rosebud aside for now.

Step 6
Take your base and your extra-large petals and begin gluing the petals to the base. Dab a few spots of glue on the bottom, the underside of the petals and press them to the outer edge of the base. Start with one petal on one side and then the next petal on the opposite side of the base.

Use two more petals to fill in the spaces between the two. Create another layer of extra-large petals, adjusting the petals so they overlap, not sit evenly on one another. Then move to the large petals, creating two layers again. Repeat the same for the medium layers. Use four small pieces to create one layer of small petals on the inside of the flower base.

Step 7
Take the remaining two small petals and glue them around your rosebud. If you want, for aesthetics, use your marker to roll the smaller petals inwards towards the rosebud.

Step 8
Apply hot glue generously to the bottom of the rosebud and press it firmly into the center of your flower base. Adjust your petal curves with your marker if you need to, but you should be ready to decorate!

Iron-On Projects

Designing Shirts

When it comes to customizing clothing, you need to consider two different aspects of the project—what you want to design and what you want to put it on. When you are first starting out working with vinyl and designs, try one-color sayings or images.

As you get more experienced, start trying on different challenges. In addition, as a beginner, start projects on cotton t-shirts. As you become more experienced, start venturing out to other clothing pieces. No matter what you choose, make sure to read the label. If the label says not to iron the article of clothing, do not try to add an iron-on to it.

If you try to add an iron-on vinyl, it will most likely ruin the clothing and your vinyl. In addition, pay attention to the fabric's stretch. As you remove the backing to your vinyl, you will be pulling on the fabric. If it is a very stretchable fabric, it will be pulled and warp under the vinyl.

Adding a bit of fusible interfacing to the inside of a stretchy piece of clothing before you add the vinyl can help prevent this.

Designing T-shirts 101

The basics of creating a t-shirt design are as follows:

1. Select the design you want to appear on the shirt.

2. In Design Space, create a new canvas to work on. Select a canvas based on the type of t-shirt you are using. Also, adjust the shirt canvas to represent the size of the shirt you will be designing.

3. Find or create the design you want to appear on the shirt and upload it onto the canvas. When you go to upload the image to the canvas, Design Space will want you to identify the type of image you are adding. The most common choice for a t-shirt design is "" simple cut."

4. Using the toolbar, choose the inside of the text or image you uploaded to let the program know that is what you want to cut out. For any words, make sure to select the inside of each letter carefully.

5. Make sure when you are done that you send the file to "cut image," not "print then cut," or your image will be printed first on the vinyl and then cut out.

6. When you see your image appears on the canvas to show you how it will appear, adjust your measurements if you feel the need.

7. Now that your design is ready to be cut, get your vinyl ready to cut. Set the dial on your machine to "iron-on" and place your vinyl on the cutting mat. Make sure to place the shiny side of the vinyl face down on the mat.

8. Select "cut" to send the design to your vinyl.

9.   Make sure to switch "mirror" prior to hitting "go."

10.   After the image is cut on your vinyl, use your weeding tool to remove any small piece of the design that needs to be removed. Remove all the extra vinyl. It is now time to attach it to the shirt.

11.   Warm up your iron, setting it to as hot as it can go. (or the linen setting) Make sure to turn off your steam function.

12.   Before placing your iron-on to your shirt, warm up your shirt with the iron for a few seconds. Doing this first will help your vinyl adhere better in the following steps.

13.   Smooth out the shirt where you want to place the design and set your vinyl over it. Lay a clean, soft cloth over the top of the iron-on to protect the plastic backing from melting onto your shirt.

14.   For 30 seconds, lay your iron over the top of the cloth and your design. Do not move the iron back and forth. If your design is larger than your iron, pick up your iron and move it to set it back down for another 30 seconds in the new spot.

      Do this until the entire design has been heated for 30 seconds by your iron. Flip the shirt over and iron the backside of the shirt directly on the other side of where your design is located. Do this for another 30 seconds per placement of your iron.

15. Turn the shirt over to the front again and take the soft cloth away. Gently peel off the plastic backing from the iron-on. It is important that you do not wait for the project to cool off! In addition, if you notice that some of the iron-on is not sticking to your shirt, place the cloth over it again and iron the spot again for another 30 seconds. Remove the iron and cloth and try removing the backing again.

16. After the backing is removed, gently pass the iron over the entire design to secure it in place.

Quilted Blanket

Project inspired by Inside Helen's Head

Quilts are a wonderful sentimental gift or keepsake. Sometimes people use them every day, while others keep them as mementos. Designing a quilt does not need to be just for children. A quilt is great to signify any occasion.

You'll need:
- Iron
- Iron-on fabric
- Cotton fabrics or a plain blanket

Step 1
In Design Space, upload or design the words or numbers you want to appear on your blanket. Select the negative spaces of the images or text and make sure to mirror your plan.

When you are choosing what to put on your project, think of things like a date, picture, or phrase. There is no limit to what you can do, just make sure it can fit on your blanket.

Step 2
Send your file to cut onto the iron-on fabric. Once it is cut, it is ready to be used. Place the image or words on your blanket where you want it to appear and then follow the instructions on your iron-on fabric and attach it with your iron.

The important part of this project is to make sure you are working on a level surface with a folded towel under the blanket. This allows a little movement to the fabric as you are working on it. This is how the edges of the iron-on fabric will adhere properly.

In addition, make sure your iron hears up to a minimum of 305 degrees Fahrenheit (150°C). Set your iron over the fabric and let it sit for 30 seconds before lifting and moving it to adhere to another area.

Matching Family Disney Shirts

Project inspired by Travelling Mom

Maybe you are planning on going on a family vacation or planning a family photo shoot. Have you started looking at matching outfits yet? Have you freaked out over the cost of trying to get you all to look great together? As a Cricut owner, you do not need to suck it up and pay the cost. All you need to do is buy an inexpensive sweatshirt or t-shirt for every member of your family and design what you want for a fraction of the cost. For this project, you can make the Disney themed shirts or any other image of your choosing.

You'll need:
- Cotton shirts for each member of your family or for each person you are making them for
- Iron-on vinyl in red and black
- Any additional embellishments you desire, like ribbon or glitter, etc.

Step 1

In Design Space, find the image of Mickey Mouse and aviator sunglasses. For the Minnie Mouse heads, add a bow shape to it.

Step 2

When you have your designs and words laid out for each shirt, send the file to cut. Make sure the heads and sunglasses are cut together from black iron-on and the bows are cut from red.

Step 3

Most likely, you will need to use your weeding tool to remove parts of the design you do not want and then peel back the rest of the negative iron-on you do not want to show up.

Step 4

Heat your iron to the hottest setting and position your vinyl on your shirts. Use the tips listed earlier in this chapter to help ensure your transfer is most successful. Test your transfer before peeling the backing off completely. Apply more heat as necessary to make sure the transfer is complete.

Step 5

When the iron-on has completely attached, peel off the plastic backing. Make sure to repeat the process for every shirt and design you made them for.

Table Runner

Project inspired by Semigloss Design

For the next holiday coming up, grab a simple set of placemats, a tablecloth or table runner, and some iron-on vinyl to set a table from the magazines. You can choose phrases, images, or shapes to correspond to any occasion or holiday. The following instructions are to help you design the image above.

You'll need:
- Black iron-on vinyl
- Tan table runner
- Iron

Step 1
In Design Space, upload two different "Day of the Dead" skulls and one rose outline. If the skulls you find do not have frames around them, also find and upload frames to places around the skulls.

Lay them out how you want them to look on your runner. Center the rose design in the middle and space the skulls and frames equally on each side.

Step 2
Send your files to cut and weed out the inside of the image that you do not want as part of your design. Remove the excess iron-on as well. Place your designs on your table runner in the locations you want them to appear and iron them on. Make sure to use a soft, clean cloth to help with the transfer.

Step 3
When the images are transferred to your runner, gently peel back the backing of the iron-on and pass your iron quickly over your designs before decorating your table.

Trendy Clutch

Project inspired by Crafting a Family

Do you want to add a little fun to your purse collection or create something special for an upcoming vacation? Pick up a fun little clutch or pouch and choose your design.

Make sure whatever clutch you pick is something you can iron on and then the options are endless! If you are feeling super crafty, maybe you want to make your own clutch! There are so many options available to you with this project.

You'll need:
- Cotton, zip-top clutch or pouch
- Teal and pink iron-on vinyl
- Iron

Step 1
With a measuring tape, measure the height and width of your clutch. This information will be used when you are in Design Space and creating your canvas to design on.

Step 2
After you create your canvas, upload your images to your workspace or design them with shapes and text on the canvas. Adjust the size so it fits nicely on the face of your bag. Once you have your image and text laid out, make sure to mirror your image for proper ironing. When you are ready, have your machine cut your iron-on. Follow the prompts and load your vinyl on our cutting mat when needed.

Step 3
Use your weeding tool to remove the negative vinyl inside your design and peel back the rest of the excess vinyl. Prepare your clutch for the image by first arming it with your iron, then centering your image and text on your bag, and covering it with a soft, clean cloth.

Place your iron on top of the cloth and let it sit for 30 seconds until you need to move it to a new place. Make sure your iron is set to its hottest setting.

Step 4
Take away the cloth and gently peel off the backing of the vinyl transfer. Pass the iron over it one last time without the cloth or backing and then start filling it up with your goodies. It is ready for you to take out and show off!

"Hangry" Apron

Project inspired by The Southern Couture

Save the day in this fun and stylish update to your kitchen apron. Use standard iron-on vinyl or more "pizazz" with glitter foil iron-on.

You'll need:
- Iron
- Soft, clean cloth
- Your choice of vinyl
- Your apron of choice

Step 1

In Design Space, open an apron file for your canvas. It might be in your best interest to measure the width and length of your apron to make sure your apron canvas is approximately the same size. It is important that you do not cut your file too large for your space on your physical apron. You can also adjust the color of the apron on this screen. This is helpful to make sure you choose a font color that compliments your apron well. You can also set the font color to the color of your vinyl.

Step 2

Open a new layer for your writing. Create a large, bold "Hangry" at the top with the part of speech and phonetic instructions in italics below "/'han-gree/ Adj." In a smaller, regular font, write out the definition, "A state of intense hunger resulting in anger and loss of self-control."

Step 3

When you are done designing your text, mirror your image. Send your file to cut by clicking on "Make It" when you are ready.

Step 4

After your file is done the cutting, use your weeding tool to remove the small pieces of vinyl that you do not want as part of your design. Peel back the other parts of vinyl you are not going to be using as well.

Step 5

Measure your apron front and determine the placement of your design on the front of your apron. Place your design on your apron with the clear liner facing towards you.

Step 6
Warm your iron to the "linen" or "cotton" setting, adjusting the heat according to the fabric you are ironing onto and the type of vinyl you are using. Lay your soft, clean pressing cloth over the top of your design.

Lay your iron over the cloth and heat the design evenly, making sure to give the vinyl plenty of time to attach itself to your apron, approximately 30 seconds for each placement of your iron.

Step 7
Once you are done pressing the front of the image, turn your apron over and press again from the backside, spending about 30 seconds per iron placement. Do not iron too long or the vinyl will begin to melt.

Step 8
Allow your design to cool and then peel away the backing, revealing your fun new addition to your trusty apron.

Sunshine the Umbrella

Project inspired by The Simply Crafted Life

Keep the rain off your head in a sweet update to your simple umbrella. No need to pay for a pricey alternative at the store when you can use a plain, inexpensive umbrella to share a beautiful and uplifting message.

You'll need
- An umbrella and an umbrella carrying bag, if provided and desired
- Yellow, or other iron-on vinyl
- Iron
- Clean, soft pressing cloth

Step 1
Determine the phrase that you want to add to your umbrella. Open Design Space and begin writing out your phrase on your canvas.

Make sure it is small enough to fit on your umbrella but large enough to be read. You may want to open your umbrella and measure the width and height where you want to place it.

Do the same for your umbrella carrying bag. This example has two different fonts: one in bold block letters and the other in a script. The image of a little sun is also added to the end of the first part of the quote. The message reads, "Create your own sunshine." You can create two versions of your saying: one large to fit on your umbrella and one smaller to fit onto your umbrella carrying case. This may require two pieces of vinyl if you are using the majority of one sheet for the umbrella saying. Also, make sure to mirror your images and words!

Step 2
Once you have your saying and any related images laid out, send the file to cut out of your yellow vinyl. Make sure you select the "kiss cut" option so the backing remains intact, but the vinyl is cut to your saying.

Step 3
Weed out any pieces on the inside of your letters or design and also remove the unnecessary vinyl from around your messages. With your umbrella open or spread out, lay your message on the outside where you want it to appear. Do the same for your carrying case and its message.

Step 4
Cover your message with your cloth and gently press for less than 30 seconds with a warm iron. Do not press too long — it is not necessary and can potentially ruin your umbrella. Work gently and quickly, making sure your image completely transfers to your umbrella and its carrying case. When you are done and the vinyl is cool, peel back the vinyl and enjoy a sunny message on a rainy day!

Monogrammed Headboard

Project inspired by A Little Craft in Your Day

A quick and trendy update to a bedroom is making this lovely monogrammed headboard. You can adjust it easily with a solid or another printed background and an image rather than a monogram if you want. In addition, it is so simple to change out that you may find yourself swapping up the look more often than not!

You'll need:
- Black iron-on vinyl
- Iron
- Clean, soft cloth for pressing
- Measuring tape
- Large striped fabric, 2 yards for a twin bed headboard
- Staple gun and staples
- Scissors for trimming the fabric
- Drill and screws
- 2 x 4's 30" long, quantity: 2
- One 56" x 33" piece of plywood
- One twin mattress topper, slightly puffy is good, kind of like an egg carton-feel

Step 1
Spread your fabric down on the floor with the printed side facing the ground, then center your mattress topper about the center of your fabric. Place the flat side of the topper down on the fabric so the bumps are facing you. Lay the plywood on top of the fabric and mattress topper about in the center.

Step 2
Using your scissors, trim the excess fabric from around the edges of the topper and wood. Leave about 2 inches of fabric on each side.

Step 3
Start on what would be the bottom of your headboard and fold the fabric and foam topper up onto the board and use your stapler and staples to securely attach the two to the wooden piece. Place your staples only an inch or two apart from one another. You do not want a lot of space between them. Next, move to the opposite side of the headboard and gently pull the fabric and foam tight as you staple them to the wood along the top of the headboard. Do the same to each side. Pay close attention to how you fold the corners, so they are secure and hidden well on the back of your headboard.

Step 4
In Design Space, create your monogram and resize it to fit well on your headboard. Make sure to mirror your monogram! When you have designed it to your liking, send the file to cut on your black vinyl by clicking on "Make It."

Once it is done the cutting, remove the extra vinyl and weed out any pieces remaining in the small spaces that you do not want as part of your design.

Step 5

Measure your headboard's height and width and locate the middle of the board. Keep in mind your headboard may dip behind your bed and frame a bit and pillows will also be stacked up against it. This means you may want your monogram to sit closer to the top, or higher up the center line of your headboard than exactly center.

Make any adjustments that you think would be most appropriate. When you find your spot, lay your monogram over and position it to your liking. Lay the cloth over top and press with a medium pressure with your warm iron. Spend about 30 seconds per press. When the vinyl is cool, gently remove the clear backing.

Step 6

Use your drill and 2 x 4's to add legs to your headboard. Measure so each leg is placed on the bottom of your headboard a few inches towards the middle, so the legs get pinned to the wall by the bed and frame. You do not want these legs to be seen.

Make sure to place your legs an equal distance from the sides so it sits correctly. When you have your placement, drill two or three screws into each leg, making sure the screws go into the wooden backing but not through the foam and fabric.

Step 7

Gently pull your bed from the wall and position your new headboard so the monogram is centered with your bed. When you have your headboard in place, push your bed back against the wall, pinning your newest focal point in place!

Vinyl – Most Versatile Medium

Christmas Ornaments

Project inspired by Hey Let's Make Stuff

If you are not thinking about the holidays in November and December, you are missing a great opportunity. It is never too early to think about gift giving. Use your Cricut machine to make gifts and decorations that everyone will enjoy.

You'll need:
- Adhesive vinyl
- Adhesive foil
- Cricut Pens
- Ornaments - plain or clear are good options

Step 1

In Design Space, upload your preferred design, image or create your own with custom shapes.

To make a dimensional design, add various layers and consider using different materials and colors to get a professional appearance.

If you want to cut words out and attach them to a strip of vinyl in another color, you can wrap that around your design. Or you could layer different vinyl, one solid and the other glitter.

Step 2

Carefully lay out your vinyl where you want it to appear on your ornament and transfer the vinyl to the ornament. Transfer tape is best for this type of project. You can use a measuring tape or ruler and a marking pen to help you find the central location for best results.

Step 3

You can have vinyl and designs attached directly to the ornaments or you can consider having pieces that hang on the outside or off of it as well. This can be a fun and personal gift, but the more you do it and practice working on a round surface, the better you will get at it!

Mason Jar Tags

Project inspired by Creativebug

Jammers rejoice! This customized label allows you to give your homemade food creations a little extra "oomph." They are incredibly easy and can fit any jar you want to use.

You'll need:
- Adhesive Vinyl in lighter colors like white or yellow
- Weeding Tool
- Transfer Tape
- Mason Jars

Step 1
Clean your jars well, especially the outside where you want to place your label. Removing as much prior residue as possible will help your new labels stick better. Also, measure the circumference and height of your jars. This way, you know which jar label canvas you need to create.

Step 2

In Design Space, open a new canvas based on the size of your mason jar that you want to create the labels for. Typically, there is a pre-set canvas. If you do not find a canvas that is the right size, open the one closest to your measurements and adjust from there.

Upload the desired images to your canvas and add any words you want to appear on the label. This can include a special message or describe the contents of the jar, etc. Make sure to detach your images so it will appear properly on your labels.

Step 3

After laying out your images and words, go back and attach all the pieces together and send your file to cut.

Step 4

After your labels are cut, weed out any unnecessary pieces and remove the excess vinyl you do not want to use. Apply the transfer tape to the vinyl and then remove the backing. Using the transfer tape, adhere the vinyl to the clean exterior of your mason jar. Smooth it with your scraper tool and then slowly peel back the tape.

Cork Coasters

Project inspired by Sewbon

Personalize your home with this sweet little project or give a gift as for a housewarming party or holiday. You can do abstract designs and words like the example or make it more personal with photos and images if you want.

You'll need:
- Cork for cutting on your Cricut
- Adhesive Vinyl
- Adhesive Felt or felt tabs
- Transfer Tape

Step 1
In Design Space, decide what size and shape of a coaster you want to create. Traditional coasters are often circular or square, but like the example shows, you do not need to be bound to those shapes for your coasters. Make sure you also have the quantity you plan to make in mind.

Step 2

When you have your design laid out, send the bottom shapes to cut out of the cork material.

Step 3

Once your cork is cut, use the coaster shapes in Design Space to now design the images, words, or other details to your coasters. You can make each coaster the same design, or you can use a theme and create custom messages for each one. It can be nice to add dates, monograms, and photographs instead of shapes and sayings. Make sure whatever you decide will fit on the coasters you just cut out.

Once you have these laid out, send your file to cut from the colored vinyl you have chosen. Weed out any unnecessary parts and then use transfer tape to move your vinyl from its backing to your project. Smooth out the vinyl with your scraper tool before removing the tape.

Step 4

Using an Exacto knife, lay your coasters on top of the adhesive felt and cut around the shape. Peel off the backing and apply the felt to the underside of the coaster. If you are using felt tabs instead, make sure there is a tab at least at every corner or few inches on the bottom of your coaster. If you want a raise coaster, you could even cut designs from the felt and add it over the vinyl on top!

It is not necessary to add the felt pieces on the bottom of the cork, but it does add a more professional touch to your project. It also adds extra protection for your furniture where you will be using the coasters.

Embellished Shoes

Project inspired by Moon Creations

There is no need to settle for "boring" or "average'" shoes anymore. And no need to let your child suffer from not knowing what foot goes to what shoe any more with this project. Adding a simple vinyl phrase or image to the soles of your shoes or even the top if you have a canvas shoe can make a big difference. To achieve this look, you will want to duplicate any images or phrases you choose or remember to make designs for both shoes, not just one!

You'll need:
- Shoes to embellish - Canvas is not necessary unless you want to iron on something to the top.
- Adhesive vinyl or iron-vinyl, depending on your design and shoe
- Transfer tape and scraper tool
- Iron, if required for iron-on

Step 1
In Design Space, create your image or phrase and send the file to cut out of the vinyl. You can use the phrase for one shoe and the negative vinyl for the other, or you can send the file to cut two times.

Step 2
Use the transfer tape to remove the vinyl design and line it up on the shoe where you want to put it. Using the scraper tool, smooth the vinyl onto the shoe. If you are adding an iron-on design, heat your iron and place your vinyl on the canvas portion of the shoe. Place a cloth over the top and iron it on.

Step 3
Carefully peel away the backing of the vinyl, making sure it has completely attached to the shoe. You can go back over your vinyl with the iron or scraper tool to make sure everything is securely in place.

Step 4
Throw on your new custom shoes and show them off to the world!

Chipboard puzzle

Project inspired by Jen Goode

When you need a fast present for a party or want to share a special moment or need to send a unique message to someone, a puzzle is a great option. Use this lovely puzzle design to make anything a bit more mysterious and special.

You can develop your own design in Design Space or upload an image already preset if you want. You can do just about anything from a pregnancy announcement to the alphabet.

You'll need:
- Chipboard
- Adhesive vinyl
- Ruler
- Masking or painter's tape

Step 1
Open Design Space and upload the image you want for your project. Make sure to create your canvas to the size of the puzzle you want to make and adjust your image to fit accordingly. There is a puzzle canvas in Design Space that you can use for the project or you can develop your own puzzle cuts if you want. If this is your first time creating the project, try out the preset cut file to get used to the process.

Step 2
Send your file to print and cut. This will first print on your vinyl and then cut the square out for the project.

Step 3
Next, you will want to place your chipboard on your cutting mat. To make sure it is secured well, use a few strips of tape to hold it on your mat for cutting.

Make marks on the chipboard before cutting one inch in on all sides. This will help you when placing your vinyl. Also, if you have a StrongGrip mat, use it for this part of the project.

Step 4
Before sending your project to cut, transfer your vinyl to the chipboard, aligning it with the marks you just made so it is in the center of the board. Go over your vinyl with your scraper tool to make sure it adheres properly.

Step 5
Adjust your cutting blade for chipboard and then send the puzzle file to cut. This will make sure the chipboard and vinyl are cut at the same time and are seamlessly aligned. If the project does not cut away the outside one-inch margin, consider painting it a corresponding color, but it should be trimmed away in the process.

Shoes Pouch

Project inspired by Atta Girl Says

Maybe it is for going to the gym, yoga, or dance, a shoe pouch is great for keeping both shoes together and neat. Plus, it makes a great gift for someone you know needs a little stylish organization in their life. You can sew this project together using a serger or straight stitch machine, or you can use liquid stitches or adhesive hem tape to enclose your project if you are not a sewer.

You'll need:
- ½ yard of the desired fabric
- Ribbon
- Thread for stitching, needle if you are doing it by hand, or another "sewing" method like liquid stitches or fusible hem tape.
- Iron-on vinyl
- Sewing materials: scissors, rotary cutter, clear quilting ruler, pins, fray check, fabric marking pen
- Iron

Step 1
Use your ruler and rotary cutter to cut the fabric in the size you want. For soft shoes, consider a rectangle like 12" by 9". For larger shoes, use maybe a rectangle about 24" by 12." Apply fray check to the edges of your fabric.

Step 2
Use your ruler to mark two spots on your fabric, 1 ½ inches from the top on each side.

Step 3
Open Design Space and prepare the image and words for your bag. Make sure your canvas is set to ½ the width of your fabric to account for the fold in the fabric.

This means you do not want anything that is larger than 9" or 12" or wider than 6" or 12," depending on the size of your fabric rectangle. Once you have your image laid out, make sure to mirror your image before sending it to cut.

Step 4
Cut your vinyl and make sure to weed away any small parts you do not want.

Step 5
Lay out your vinyl on your fabric, sticky side down on the print side of your fabric. Do not lay your design about ½" from the bottom or sides of your fabric to account for the seam you are going to create. Also, keep it about one inch from the top to account for the ribbon loop you are going to create. Once you have it laid out, use a pressing cloth and your iron to attach your vinyl to your fabric.

Step 6
After you adhere your vinyl to your project, fold your fabric in half and align the edges, pinning them in place. Sew along the edge to secure the bag shape. If you are using another means of making the bag, follow the directions on the packaging. Make sure to fold the fabric in ½ inch to enclose the raw edges of the fabric. Do not sew or close off the top of your bag. Also, do not sew beyond the markings you made with your pen earlier.

Step 7
Fold the edge of the top of your bag down. You can make a little fold, about ¼ inch, and then fold again at ¾ inch to encase the seam allowance, or just fold it down one inch and sew it closed. Again, if you are not sewing your project, use your closure material to create the ribbon casing for closing the bag. Do not close off the ends of the bag, making a tube for the ribbon to pass through.

Step 8
Cut a length of ribbon three or more inches longer than the unfinished width of your bag, meaning 15" or "28". Apply fray check to the ends of the ribbon. Thread the ribbon through the ribbon casing or tube you just created. Attaching a safety pin to one end of the ribbon and using that to pass the ribbon through can be helpful in this process. You want the ribbon coming out on one side of the bag for you can clinch it closed and tie a bow to keep the shoes inside.

Step 9
Consider adding a new pair of shoes or a special treat inside the bag if you are giving it as a gift or simply slide your shoes on and take them with you in their stylish new casing!

Sleeping Mask

Project inspired by Bespoke Bride

Another "sewing" project that you can make with your Cricut is a sleeping mask to help block out unwanted light. These are great for traveling and times when you need some shut-eye but the sun is still shining. Like the previous project, you can sew this with a sewing machine or serger, or you can use liquid stitching or iron-on hem tape to capture the look you are going for.

You'll need:
- Printed or solid top fabric, such as cotton quilting fabric
- Silky or Minky fabric for the underside of the mask that sits over your eyes
- 13 inches of wide, good-quality elastic
- iron-on vinyl in corresponding color, like black
- Sewing materials: scissors, rotary cutter, clear quilting ruler, pins, fray check, fabric marking pen

Step 1
To begin, start with the vinyl image you want on the outside of your eye mask. This can be a word or a graphic. Design the image on Design Space, making sure that the image will fit on an eye mask. In general, you do not want an image longer than four inches or higher than two inches. Once you have your design laid out, send the file to be cut from your vinyl. When the image is done cutting, weed it if necessary and prepare it to be transferred to the eye mask.

Step 2
If you are making your own mask by hand, create the eye mask pattern on paper. You can also do this in Cricut, making the eye mask shape and cutting it on paper. Lay your pattern over your two different fabrics, placing the right sides of the fabrics together. Pin the pattern down and cut it out with a rotary cutter. If you want your own custom mask, use your face measurements to adjust your pattern.

Step 3
Once you have your top mask cut out, lay your vinyl design on it and press it onto the mask. Make sure to use the "cotton" setting on your iron and place a pressing cloth or a soft, clean cloth in between your design and the iron.
Before you remove the backing, make sure your vinyl is fully transferred. Once the backing is removed, pass your iron over the design one more time.

Step 4
Lay the bottom, minky or silky fabric on the cutting table with the fashion side or right side of the fabric facing you. Pin one end of the elastic to one side of the material in the center of the eye mask and then bring the other end to the opposite side of the mask, pinning that end in place, too.

Pin it so the end is facing out of your fabric. Let about one inch of elastic hang over the edge on each side.

Once the elastic is secured, place your top fabric with the vinyl design on top of the minky or silky fabric, placing the design down away from you. Use more pins to attach the two pieces of fabric together and prepare the project for sewing. If you are not sewing your project, skip directly to the alternative step.

Step 5
Using your sewing machine or a needle and thread, stitch the edges of your eye mask together, leaving a two-inch space on the top, straight edge of your mask.

Keep the opening at least one inch away from your elastic — the further, the better. Make sure to back stitch over the elastic area to give it more support.

Step 6
When you are done sewing, turn your project right side out by pressing it through the open space you left open. Your mask should look almost complete, but with a two-inch gap still visible. Press the edges of the opening inside the mask and use a needle and thread to close the hole in the mask.

If you press it with an iron first, it will help keep all the loose and raw edges contained while you are sewing it closed. If you want to add a decorative top stitch to your design, stitch around ¼ inch from the edge. This will also stabilize your design. Once you are done, press with an iron.

Amended Step
For those that do not want to sew the project, you can press the raw edges in on the minky and fashion fabric with your iron.

Use a piece of fusible interfacing cut out in the shape of the eye mask but trimmed by ½ inch around the edges. Lay that on the wrong side of your minky or silky fabric and place your fashion fabric on top, with the design facing you. Set your iron on the fabric, with a pressing cloth in between.

Add extra interfacing to where you inserted the elastic to add more stability. Make sure the interfacing fully adheres the layers together and that the elastic is secured in place.

Leather Designs

You do not need to worry—this is all about the faux leather materials that Cricut offers for your crafting needs now. What is great about this material is how versatile it is.

You can make projects from jewelry to home décor and more. It offers the look and feel of real leather, but on one side, it has the leather texture and on the other, it is faced with soft felt. You can also purchase different textures for the leather, like pebbled, suede, and wood grain! If you are not sure what you want to commit to just yet, buy a sampler pack to check out the different colors and textures yourself.

Typically, a sample pack will offer one sheet of five different textures that measures about 12" x 12". A roll of faux leather usually is a single sheet of 12"x 24" of a single texture. The sampler pack also gives you a variety of colors when you order it. If you are doing a big project, consider getting a roll of leather, but sampler packs are awesome for smaller projects like jewelry.

The benefit of this material to Cricut users is that you do not need to buy a new blade to cut through it. The standard blade with your machine should cut through this material. In addition, this material is a fraction of the cost of a real leather material.

Because it does not require additional blades or attachments, you can use this material with just about any Cricut machine! When you are planning a leather project, you can think traditional, like earrings, bracelets, and catch-all's, or out of the box, like pillows and purses. You can also add bits of faux leather to paper designs like cards and scrapbook pages.

The process of cutting faux leather is easy. When you send your design to cut from Design Space, you place the material on your cutting mat. Place your cutting mat in your machine and set your dial to "custom." If you have the option in Design Space, specify the material as "Leather, Faux – 1mm (Cricut)." Also, a sticky StandardGrip cutting mat works for this material, but if it has lost a bit of stickiness, try using a StrongGrip cutting mat instead.

Also, the felt of the backing can leave fuzz on the mat, which is hard to remove. To combat this, try cutting your projects with the leather side facing down on your mat. If you plan on doing this, always mirror your image before sending it to cut.

Also, if you are making a design that shows the backside of the material and do not want the felt to show, cut a mirror of the project and glue the second piece on the back of the project. Make sure to use a strong and permanent adhesive to make sure the two pieces stay together for a long time.

Leather Feather Pendant Necklace

Project inspired by It Happens in a Blink

This is a simple and trendy project that you can change up according to the colors you want and the shape you desire. This feather design is an evergreen style with a mix of rustic orange and metallic gold. Try different shapes like abstract images and other color palettes like silver, green, etc.

You'll need:
- Painter's tape
- Golden paint
- Paintbrush
- Faux leather in pebbled texture and in an orange color
- Jewelry kit, such as rings and chain
- Something to poke a hole in the leather for the ring, such as a thick needle

Step 1

In Design Space, create an outline of the feather design you wish to be your pendant. Readjust the sizing to be as large or as small as you want. To prevent the felt side from showing, create two images of this shape and mirror one of the images.

Step 2

When your design is ready, send your fit to cut on your faux leather. You can load the material with the texture side on the mat and the felt facing up because you are cutting two shapes already mirrored.

Step 3

Use a strip of painter's tape, mark off a line on your leather pieces about halfway up the feather. Paint the lower portion of the feather with your gold paint. Allow to dry and remove the paint. To get the best results, use your scraper tool over the tape to make sure it has well adhered to your leather piece.

Step 4

Once the pieces are dry completely, use a permanent adhesive to attach the two feather pieces to one another, enclosing the felt back between the layers. Fabric fusion is a good adhesive to consider. Follow the directions on the bottle to get the best results.

Step 5

Use a sharp, large needle to poke a hole in the top of the feather and slide the jewelry ring through it. Attach it to the chain and get ready to rock your newest leather accessory!

Leather Cuff Bracelet

Project inspired by Printable Crush

Add a little charm to your wrist this year with a custom leather cuff bracelet or make a few to give out as presents for birthdays and other special occasions. They are stylish and comfortable, a winning combination!

You'll need:
- Hot glue gun
- Faux leather in pebbled texture and rich brown color
- Measuring tape
- Scissors

Step 1
Measure around your wrist and write down the measurement.

Step 2

In Design Space, create a new workspace and create a rectangle about 1 ½ inches wide and the length of your wrist plus two inches long. For example, if your wrist is seven inches around, you would add two inches to that measurement, and design your rectangle nine inches long.

Step 3

Add a shape, such as a triangle, to your rectangle shape in the center. Create three shapes if you want to create the example above. Attach all three together and then align them in the center horizontally and vertically by clicking on "Attach" and then "Align."

Step 4

Create two smaller rectangles about two inches by ¼ inch. When all the pieces are created, send the file to cut. Play your material on your mat and follow the prompts.

Step 5

Remove your pieces from the mat, including removing the inside little triangles, and use a dab of glue to turn the two small rectangles into loops that go around the larger rectangle. Glue the loops to the large bracelet rectangle towards the end of one side. Trim the other side at an angle. This helps the end slide in and out easier.

Leather Earrings

Project inspired by Everyday Jenny

Kind of like the leather feather necklace, this project uses a metallic accent over the leather to add a little drama to the jewelry, but this time instead of paint, the project calls for iron-on adhesive! This is a great project to try your hand at the iron-on with the faux leather and then you will know which process you prefer to get a similar look.

You'll need:
- Iron-on vinyl in rose gold
- Faux leather in cream pebbled texture
- Earring kit and materials
- Sharp needle
- Adhesive to attach your earrings front and back pieces, such as Fabric Fusion.

Step 1

In Design Space, begin laying out your pieces. Create four exact teardrops—two pieces will be glued together back to back so the felt side does not show.

Step 2

Decide how you want the vinyl to be added to your project and create those images now. You can use the "Slice and Weld" option to help you get good angles and precise pieces.

Step 3

When your project is laid out, send the files to cut. Load your leather material with the texture side facing down and the felt side facing up. Follow the prompts on when to add your vinyl.

Step 4

Remove all your pieces. Glue the front and back of the earrings together. Position your vinyl over your earring pieces and place a soft, clean cloth over the top. Lay your iron over the top and press until the vinyl adheres to the leather. Do not set your iron to the "cotton" setting, but maybe just a few notches lower. Press for about 30 seconds. Remove the backing after the project cools a bit.

Step 5

Use your needle to puncture holes in the top of the earring pieces and then insert the earring hardware through the holes to make your earrings.

Wooden Designs

Rustic-chic Signs

Project inspired by Cherished Bliss

Any piece of wood works to create a beautiful, custom sign. You do not need to do much beyond attaching vinyl, but you can get as creative as you want with it!

You'll need:
- Adhesive Vinyl – any color
- Transfer Tape
- Wood for the base of the sign
- Paint, if desired.

Step 1
If you want to, paint the base of wood whatever color you have chosen. Most common colors are ivory or pastel colors. You can also stain your wood. Allow time for it to dry. Also, you can leave the edges of your wood rough or sand them for a smoother look.

Step 2

In Design Space, upload your image or create your phrase that you want to appear on your sign. Make sure to adjust your canvas to be the size of your sign so that you create images that fit your project best. If you are making a big sign, tell your machine to break so you can load more vinyl. The best way to do this is to add a colored square.

Step 3

Tell your machine to cut your design when you are ready. Follow the prompts on the screen to load materials as needed. When it is done cutting, weed out all the little spaces you do not want and peel away the unnecessary vinyl.

Step 4

Use transfer tape to help you move the vinyl design from the provided backing to your project. Lay your design on your wood and use your scraper tool to attach the vinyl to your base. For best results, consider using a pencil and ruler to make sure everything is aligned properly. Once you have your vinyl placed, use your scraper tool to securely attach your design, removing all air bubbles. Peel off the transfer tape and get ready to display your new sign.

If you are hanging your sign on the wall, purchase a picture hanging kit from the hardware store and follow the instructions in the kit to add a hanging device to the back of the project. Enjoy!

Wooden Airplane Décor

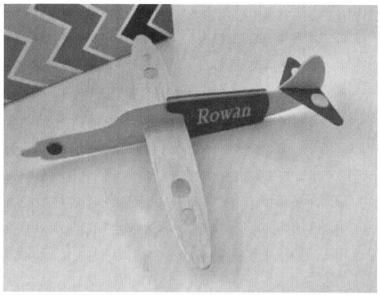

Project inspired by Carole's Cricut Crafts

More and more wooden projects are popping up in Design Space, and this cool airplane is just one of them. You can choose the wood you work with, but balsa wood continues to be a favorite for Cricut projects. This material is not only thinner and less expensive than other options, it is also a lot easier to find!

You'll need:
- Two pieces of 1/32-inch thick balsa wood
- Dark stain
- Ivory adhesive vinyl
- Super glue or wood glue

Step 1

This is a "Make it Now" project in Design Space so open the library, search for the project, and open the project in a new workspace. Using a StrongGrip cutting mat, lay your balsa wood pieces on and make sure to adjust your settings to "custom" on your machine. When you are ready, send your project to cut. If the machine does not cut through the first time, repeat cutting, without moving your mat, three or four more times.

Step 2

Gently remove the wood pieces from your mat. This is a fragile wood, so be very careful removing the pieces so you do not break them. Lay your pieces to the side for now.

Step 3

Go back to Design Space and write out the name or message you want to appear on the side of the plane. Make sure the size is correct for the size of the plane. Add your vinyl to your StandardGrip cutting mat and tell your machine to cut the image. Follow the prompts on your computer.

Step 4

Weed out the insides of your vinyl as necessary and remove the unnecessary exterior vinyl that is not part of your design. When it is ready, lay the design on your airplane and use the scraper tool to transfer the vinyl to the corresponding piece.

Step 5

You can offer the pieces of the plane with instructions as a gift, or you can assemble the plane yourself. If you are making it, use your super glue or wood glue to securely attach all the pieces to one another and allow them to dry fully. Place this design somewhere people can enjoy your handiwork!

Wood Dangle Earrings

Project inspired by Three Little Monkeys Studio

These earrings are versatile and customizable. It is easiest if you have a Xyron 1.5" sticker maker with a permanent adhesive, but you can achieve the same results without it. Just make sure you add enough adhesive and allow time for drying.

You'll need:
- Earring metal pieces
- Foam roller
- Xyron 1.5" sticker maker and permanent adhesive or another permanent adhesive
- Orange, pink, and gold acrylic paint
- Wood finishing cloths or wood stain
- Painter's tape
- Wood veneer cardstock

Step 1
In InDesign, create a teardrop shape. If you do not have InDesign, open Design Space and look through the shapes and images until you find a shape that resembles a teardrop or surfboard. Remove all the layers until it is an outline. Repeat the outline or shape 12 times, making sure it fits on the cardstock sheet.

You can tell your Cricut to cut 12 of the images when you go to cut it, and this allows the machine to replicate the image and optimize your cardstock for you! If you do not have a "wood" setting, set your machine to "cardstock," especially if your veneer is thin.

Step 2
If you are using the Xyron machine, place ten of your cuts into the machine and apply adhesive to the backs. This leaves two without adhesive. Begin sandwiching the pieces together, five to each earring.

Place one cut without adhesive on the back of each pile. This means each earring has six layers of veneer. If you do not have this machine, apply a thin layer of adhesive to the back of ten of your boards, working quickly as you layer each earring, ending with a sixth piece that does not have adhesive on the back.

Step 3
Using your stain, apply two coats to the front, back, and sides of both earrings. Make sure to let them dry overnight so the stain can set properly. If you prefer a lighter or darker look, adjust the number of coats you apply to your liking.

Step 4

Place your painter's tape over your earrings to mark where you want to paint. The tape will make sure the lines remain sharp and precise.

You can hand paint without the tape if you want a more DIY look. Begin with the top color, in this example the gold color, and then move to the pink, and end with the orange. Give some time for drying in between each application. Depending on your color choices and paint quality, you may need to do two or more coats. Also, make sure to paint with the grain of your wood for the best results.

Step 5

Using your reamer tool, poke a hole in the top of the earrings where the hardware is going to go. You can press through more to widen the whole as needed. If you have a bead reamer, you can use that, too.

Step 6

Once your holes are wide enough, press your earring hardware through on each earring and secure in place! Now you are ready to wear or gift a beautiful pair of wooden earrings.

Mini Christmas Trees

Project inspired by A Cup of Thuy

This simple project can add a sophisticated touch to your holiday décor or table place settings. If you want to change these up a little bit, consider adding your guest's names along one side of the design before cutting.

This personalized touch will bring your holiday dinner party from good to glam in a heartbeat! If you want to keep the project as it is, make up a bunch of these trees and place them in groups to make a beautiful and custom focal point.

You'll need:
- Spray adhesive
- Ruler
- Exacto or crafting knife
- Glitter tape or glitter paint
- Matching patterned fabric
- 3mm thick balsa wood
- The predesigned Christmas tree patterns in Design Space

Step 1

Open up the patterns in Design Space. Make sure to create both sizes for variety in height. Click "Make It" and follow the prompts. You may need to send it to print a few times to cut the image completely through the balsa wood.

If you are making placeholders for your table, make sure to write and add your names on your cuts now before cutting your images out. You can write them with the pen, although depending on your wood it can come out a little rough. Another option is to print the names in vinyl and apply them after cutting.

Step 2

Use your Exacto knife to finish any cuts necessary. Remove the outside, excess wood.

Step 3

Spray one side of your tree pieces and lay them flat on your fabric, pressing down firmly to make sure the fabric adheres evenly to your design. Let the adhesive dry completely. *Review step 5 before attaching your fabric in the event you are working with glitter paint later in the project.

Step 4
Working with your Exacto knife, trace around your tree shapes to cut away all the extra fabric. If you want to repeat steps 3 and 4 on the other side of the trees, you can have completely decorated trees. If you do not, the back side of the trees will be wooden while the fronts will have patterned, like the image above.

Step 5
Using your Exacto knife, trim your glitter tape to 3mm, or purchase your tape 3mm wide. Wrap the tape around the edges of all the tree pieces, pressing to secure it. If you are using glitter paint, carefully apply the paint to the edge of all the trees and allow to dry. If you are not steady with a paintbrush, consider doing this step before adhering your fabric so any mistakes will be covered by the added fabric.

Step 6
Once all the pieces are designed and dry, slip the bottom cuts into the top, pressing down so the "trunk" of the trees sit evenly on your flat surface. You are ready to decorate!

Woodland Drink Charms

Project inspired by Albion Gould

Wine charms can be pricey, especially if you want something more custom to an event or personality. Instead of spending a fortune for a sweet wedding memento or making a dinner party stand out, consider making your own! The process is simple and the options are endless!

You'll need:
- 3mm thick balsa wood
- inexpensive "silver" hoop earrings in the number of charms you want to make
- Variety of paints, such as brown, green, orange, etc.

Step 1

Open Design Space and insert various images you want to turn into wine charms. Keep the size smaller so that they will not interfere with someone holding the wine glass, but large enough to be able to identify easily. Add a small circle to each shape that will be cut out and where you will end up attaching the earring too.

Step 2

Cut the shapes onto the balsa wood. You may need to send it to cut a few times to make sure it has cut all the way through your wood.

Step 3

Remove the outside, extra wood, and weed out the circle from each shape.

Step 4

Paint your shapes or stain them in the colors you want. Allow them to dry completely.

Step 5

Once dry, thread one earring through the hole and get ready to dress up your next beverage! Consider adding initials, monograms, images, and patterns to the wine charms for different occasions.

Wooden Gift Tags

Project inspired by Dossier Blog

Kick up your gift giving a notch this year with these wooden tags. Handwrite the names on or add a vinyl custom message to the tag, if you want.

You'll need:
- Paint in your preferred colors, such as pink, black, white, etc.
- Painter's tape
- Hole punch, single is best
- Exacto or crafting knife
- 1mm this balsa wood
- Twine or thin ribbon

Step 1
In Design Space, create the gift tag shape you want to create. You can do a shape like the image above, or a circle, or standard rectangle. You can also adjust the size to match the size of the package as well. Try creating a variety of shapes and sizes to see what ones you prefer and to make your packages all unique. When you have placed the shapes on your workspace, add small circles that will be cut out for threading your twine or ribbon through.

Step 2

Send your file to be cut, making a couple passes over the wood if necessary. This thickness should not require too many extra cuts to get all the way through.

Step 3

Remove the extra wood from the outside of your tags and the interior circles.

Step 4

Apply the painter's tape to the bottom edge of your tag to mark off where you want to paint. Apply one or two layers of paint to your tags and let it dry completely.

Step 5

When you are ready to use your tags, cut off a piece of the ribbon or twine and thread it through the whole. Tie it on your package and write your recipient's name or custom message!

Etching on Glass and Metal

If you have made a stencil out of vinyl before, then you can etch on glass and metal. The process is very similar. The main difference is that with a traditional vinyl sticker, you are using paint to create a design, while with etching, you are using a different solution to get the results. On metal, it can be a little different, but the concept is still the same.

As you begin this project, keep in mind that simple is always best when starting out. Choose a design with larger spaces and less intricate details. Usually, the best vinyl for an etching project is stencil vinyl. The reason this is great is because the backing material is designed to stay solid while the project is being cut. This is called a "kiss" cut. You can use other types of vinyl for etching projects, but it may not turn out the best because not all vinyl is great at keeping the etching solution away from the glass or metal. Thickness is usually the key factor in determining your success. If you want to try it out, do a test cut before you use your final vinyl for the project.

The "kiss cut" referred to earlier is a cutting adjustment you can make on your machine. It allows the machine to cut the vinyl but not all the way through the backing material. Below are some directions for different Cricut machines to help you adjust the cutting settings for the "kiss cut."

- **Create**: Blade depth #3, Pressure Medium Speed High, Multi-cut 1, blade assembly regular
- **Expression**: Blade depth #3, Pressure Medium Speed High, Multi-cut 1, blade assembly regular
- **Expression 2**: Blade depth #3, Pressure Medium Speed High, Multi-cut 1, blade assembly regular
- **Imagine**: Blade depth #3, Pressure #3, Speed High, Multi-cut 1, blade assembly regular

- **Mini**: Blade depth #3, Pressure #2, Speed High, Multi-cut 1, blade assembly regular
- **Explore**: "Custom" Smart Dial, Material "Stencil Vinyl," select 0.2 mm (Cricut)

Prior to sending your file to cut, add a strip of vinyl to your cutting mat with the backing facing up. Place your project vinyl over the top. When finished with your design, weed away any leftover pieces.

To make sure your vinyl is attached well, place it on your project and smooth it out with your scraper tool in a circular motion so the air bubbles are removed.

Stir your etching cream well before applying it to your project. Also, make sure to read the instructions on your cream well before using it.

Use a foam brush to apply a thick coating of the cream to your project over the stencil. Do not use a brush with bristles because it will apply unevenly. Allow enough time to dry, according to the package.

Once your project is dry and it looks like it has done something to your material, rinse your project in clean water in a sink. Use a soft sponge to help remove any lingering cream. Make sure the sponge is used only from crafting and the sink is free from dishes, etc. Sometimes when the project is wet, you do not see the etching. Allow the project to dry to see the result. Consider leaving the stencil on until it dries to make sure it has done its job.

You do not need to restrict yourself to just glass. Any smooth surface can be etched on. The best way to get inspired on what to etch will be listed as etch-able materials on the container of your etching cream.

Etched Glass Casserole Dish

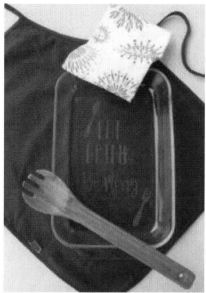

Project inspired by Hello Creative Family

If you are responsible for bringing food to a party, why not make it personal? Add a little message to the bottom of your dish, or your name, to make sure your host knows that you appreciate the invitation, and who to return the dish to when it is done!

You'll need:
- 9x13" glass baking dish
- Etching cream and application brush
- Stencil vinyl
- Rubber gloves
- Transfer Tape

Step 1

In Design Space, add your words and graphics that you want to have cut from the stencil vinyl. In this example, the words are "Eat, Drink, Be Merry" with a spoon and fork image. Adjust them to fit on the bottom of the dish, no bigger than 12" or wider than 8". Make sure to mirror your design for easier application!

Step 2

Once your design is laid out, click on "Make It" and follow the prompts to cut it from the stencil vinyl.

Step 3

Weed out your design and using your transfer tape, place the negative vinyl onto the bottom of your baking dish. Make sure to use your scraper to get the sticky side of the stencil to attach smoothly to the bottom of your dish, paying close attention to the little parts of the design. Also, do not place the image on the bottom of the dish where food will be placed, but rather on the underside of the dish so it shows through the glass but does not come in contact with food.

Step 4

Remove the transfer tape and follow the directions on the bottle of etching cream you purchased. Wear your rubber gloves and use your application brush! Let dry appropriately.

Step 5

Keeping your rubber gloves on, remove the excess etching cream. This usually requires washing it off in the sink with a paper towel or soft cloth. Pat dry and then peel off the stencil. Enjoy!

Superhero Beer or Drinking Glasses

Project inspired by I am Momma Hear Me Roar

Capture the attention and the heart of your superhero-loving friend or partner with a set of these custom beer or drinking glasses. It is easy to do, and inexpensive, too! Check the dollar store for the perfect glass to work with if you do not have some already!

You'll need:
- Several smooth, glass drinking glasses
- Etching cream and application brush
- Stencil vinyl
- Rubber gloves
- Transfer Tape

Step 1
In Design Space, search for superhero logos. Remove the extra layers so they are only the outlines. Make as many logos as your glasses count. This means if you have six glasses, choose six logos to print. Send your file to cut on the stencil vinyl by clicking on "Make It." Follow the prompts to cut. Do not forget to mirror your images!

Step 2

Once your images cut in the vinyl, weed out the interior pieces, making sure to keep the little pieces in tact! Working with one logo at a time, transfer the logo with the transfer tape to a glass. Use your scraper tool to make sure there are no air bubbles and it is firmly attached to the glass. Repeat this for each logo.

Step 3

Remove the transfer tape and follow the instructions on your etching cream. Allow to dry the appropriate time. Make sure to use your rubber gloves and application brush.

Step 4

Wearing your rubber gloves, wash off the excess etching cream with a paper towel or soft, clean cloth. Pat dry and remove the vinyl carefully. Now get ready for awe and appreciation!

Etched Metal Necklace Charms

Project inspired by The Vinyl Cut

If you are a proud owner of Cricut Explore or Explore Air, you have the great option of using the metal etching tool! This handy little attachment simply loads into your machine and offers metal etching at the push of the button.

You'll need:
- Metal etching or engraving tool for your machine
- Various metal charms, 24 gauge, 9/16" and ½" diameter, silver or gold-plated copper
- Stencil vinyl

Step 1
In Design Space, create a circle the size of your metal charm. Add your image to your canvas and remove all the extra layers so only the outline exists. Scale the image and place it inside your circle.

Step 2
Send the file to cut on vinyl first. When the vinyl is done cutting, remove the circle cut and place your metal disc inside the circle. This ensures your disc is placed in exactly the correct spot.

You can cover the disc with another piece of vinyl if you are worried about it sliding on your mat during the cut, or you can place your vinyl piece upside down on your mat and then only remove the paper backing after the cut so the stick part remains.

From here, you can attach your metal circles to the sticky spot that will be etched. Once you have your disc positioned, send the file to engrave, this time on the metal disc.

Step 3
If you do not want just an outline, consider filling in the lines and sending it to etch. This will create straight lines across the image, which can make it more distinguished than just the outline on the metal. When it is done, place it on a ribbon or chain and wear or gift!

Etched Metal Coasters

Project inspired by Dan the Maker Man on Instructables

For those that do not have the ability to add an etching tool to their machine, it does not mean you cannot also experience the joy of metal etching! It does mean you need to get a little messy and pick up a special chemical, Ferric Chloride, but it is doable and fast. You can purchase this chloride at an electronics store or online. The great news is that you can use the liquid for multiple projects!

You'll need:
- Ferric Chloride
- Metal coasters or squares
- Foam adhesive circles
- Rubber gloves
- Rubbermaid container large enough to fit the coasters lying down and the chloride solution
- Stencil, adhesive vinyl
- Transfer Tape

Step 1

In Design Space, design your images to be etched onto your coasters. Make sure they are stencils, so remove all design except for the outline of the image. Create a square just slightly larger than the size of your coaster. Place your image in the square and then send the image to cut.

Step 2

When the image is cut, weed out the inside of the image, leaving the outer square on the paper backing. Use your transfer tape to remove one square with your image from the backing and place it on a metal coaster. The vinyl should hang off the edges just a little bit. Use your scraper tool to adhere the vinyl well to the coaster and then remove the transfer tape. Do this for all the coasters you are making.

Step 3

Mix up your Ferric Chloride in your Rubbermaid container. It is typically a 1-part chloride, 1-part water ratio. Wear your gloves and do not use a spoon for stirring that you want to use again for eating!

Step 4

Working with one coaster at a time and wearing your rubber gloves, slip the coaster into the chloride. Make sure the top of the coaster with the vinyl sticker is facing up and completely covered with the solution. Let the coaster sit for 30 minutes.

Step 5

Still wearing your gloves, remove the coaster from the solution and rinse in clean water to remove the excess solution. Use a soft cloth or paper towels to rub off the excess still clinging on. Remove the vinyl stencil and throw it away. If you have a black ash-like residue still sticking to the exposed metal, lightly sand the surface with a 1200 grit sandpaper.

Step 6

On the underside of the coaster, attach the foam circles to the corners to protect the table surfaces from being scratched by the metal. If you prefer, you can use spray adhesive and foam sheets to cover the entire bottom of the coaster in foam. You can then use an Exacto or craft knife to trace around the coaster, cutting away the extra foam.

Various other projects

Traffic Light Chart

The _____ Family Traffic Light Chart

Project inspired by C'mon, Get Crafty!

Parenting is hard and having good tools to help encourage good behavior are critical. Being a teacher is hard and keeping kids in line and making good decisions is hard, too! Using a behavior chart is a good method for keeping a visual system that is easy to follow for just about any child.

You'll need:
- Grey or black cardstock
- Green, yellow, and red adhesive vinyl
- Magnetic sheets
- Hot glue

Step 1

Buy the traffic light template from Pixar Car, or design your own. The basic shapes used in the design are rectangle and circles. Play around with the shapes and lines until you have a template that you want to use. In addition, the center of each major rectangle should have a large circle to be cut from the metal and different colored vinyl. If you want to add text like the example, add the words to be printed on your vinyl or cut out of black vinyl and then layered on top. When you are ready, send your file to cut and follow the prompts to load your mats with the cardstock, magnet sheets, and vinyl.

Step 2

When you are cutting your magnet, you can choose to cut the vinyl and magnet separately, print directly onto the magnetic surface, or attach the vinyl to the metal and then cut the two together. When you add vinyl to your magnetic material, use your scraper tool to make sure it is applied evenly and without air bubbles.

Step 3

Apply glue to the back of each circle and place it in the traffic light background, making sure the red is on top and the green is on the bottom. If you added additional vinyl words to the circles, make sure to add them at this point, too.

Step 4

If you do not have magnets for the children already, you can make some for your board. Use the magnetic materials to design a custom magnet for each person or glue other objects to pieces of magnet to use on the board. Things like plastic animals, wooden initials, and full names on Popsicle sticks work well.

Step 5

Add a few strips of magnetic or another hanging mechanism on the back of the traffic light to help hang it on the wall or other magnetic surfaces, like the fridge. Now you have a great tool for encouraging good behavior all day long!

Welcome Bags

Project inspired by Lydia Out Loud

When your big day approaches, it is customary to offer out-of-town guests a little wedding welcome bag full of goodies that they may find useful, like Advil, stain remover, and other handy "recovery" items. Instead of just throwing them into any old bag, add a custom flair to show how much you care and thought about them, even on your wedding day.

Choose materials and colors based on your own wedding colors and theme. This project is based on the state of Ohio and the colors teal and gold. The directions that follow are for the bag, door hanger, water bottle wrap, thank you card, and luggage tag.

Most of the base supplies are available at the Dollar Store, including the little items you want to stock in the bag as well. Not only is this a thoughtful and elegant touch, but it can be inexpensive, too!

Custom Gift Bag

What you'll need:
- Cardstock in the main color of your wedding
- Sticky vinyl in the secondary color of your wedding
- Adhesive runner used for scrapbooking
- Sticky foam mounts
- Thick ribbon in complimentary colors to your wedding colors

Step 1
Make or find a state cut file and download it into Design Space. Add any text you want, like "Welcome" or "Jim and Jo's Wedding Weekend."

Step 2
Load your cardstock on your cutting mat and cut out your state shape. Set your dial to "Light Cardstock" for the best results.

Step 3

Load your sticky foil onto your mat and cut out your text. Set your dial to "custom" for best results. Use your weeding tool to remove the negative space you do not want to be a part of your design.

Step 4

Transfer your wording to your state shape. Use your scoring tool to make sure it is well attached. Gently pull away the backing materials.

Step 5

Place a strip of adhesive tape to the inside of the bag, between the handles and on the underside of the bag on the same side. Measure the length, add a ½ inch to your measurement, and cut that length of ribbon. Attach the ribbon to the bag, using the adhesive strips to secure it down. You can also place adhesive strips along the ribbon's edge to make sure it sticks to the front of the bag as well, but do not do this until you have positioned the ribbon to your liking.

Step 6

On the back of the state shape, attach several of the foam mounts evenly around the border of the shape. Turn the shape over and center it on your bag. When you find the right location, press it down firmly around the border, making sure to press each foam mount so it attaches securely to the bag. If you decide you do not want a raised shape, you can add the scrapbooking adhesive strips along the back of the shape and press it firmly into place instead.

Personal Door Hanger

What you'll need:
- Cardstock in the main color of your wedding
- Sticky vinyl in the secondary color of your wedding
- Sparkling cardstock, if matches your wedding theme
- Adhesive runner used for scrapbooking

Step 1
In Design Space, load the "Door Hanger" template from the Design Space Library. This will be about 3.5 inches wide and 8.5 inches high. Place your cardstock on your mat and cut out the door hanger.

Step 2
Write out the words you want to appear on your door hanger and adjust them to fit on the design. You can say something like, "Shhhhh - We're recovering from partying last night at Jim and Jo's Wedding," or "Quiet Time after Party Time at Jim and Jo's wedding." Print and cut your words from the sticky vinyl.

Step 3
Attach your words to your door hanger in the location you prefer. Use your scraper tool to firmly adhere the vinyl to the cardstock. Gently peel away the backing for the foil when you are certain the words are securely attached.

Step 4
If you are adding glitter, cut a few pieces from the width of your door hanger and attach them to the back of the door hanger with adhesive running tape. This step is optional, but it does help it become sturdier.

Step 5
Cut the circle apart on the bottom of the circle near the side of the hanger so it can easily fit over a handle or a knob.

Matching Water Bottle Label

What you'll need:
- Sticky vinyl in white or primary color
- Sticky foil in your secondary color

Step 1
Mark and cut the white vinyl or primary-colored vinyl into strips. A traditional label is about seven inches long and 2 ½ inches wide. Measure your water bottle labels for an accurate size for your project.

Step 2
In Design Space, create a custom monogram or write out the wording for your label. You can include your new monogram or information like, "Jim and Jo's Wedding Weekend 2019." Print and cut the words on the sticky foil in your secondary color. Use your weeding tool to remove any negative space that is not part of your design. Transfer your monogram or words to your vinyl. Use your scraping tool to make sure it adheres well.

Step 3
Remove the white vinyl backing and wrap the label around your bottles. It looks so much nicer than throwing a regular bottle into your bag! If you have the time and the desire, consider making wraps for other items in your bag as well, such as tissue packages or gum boxes.

A Handmade Thank You Card

What you'll need:
- Cardstock in the main color of your wedding
- Sparkling cardstock, if matches your wedding theme, or cardstock in your secondary color
- Acetate paper liners for the envelope liners
- Adhesive runner used for scrapbooking

Step 1

In Design Space, open the card and envelope template. Place your main color cardstock on your cutting mat and the scoring blade into the machine next to your cutting blade and cut your card. Use your weeding tool to remove any parts that remain that you do not want.

Step 2

Trim your sparkling cardstock to the size of the thank you card top part and attach it to the underside of your card top with adhesive scrapbooking tape. You want to put this piece of cardstock under your cut-out design so the sparkle shows through.

Step 3

Add the cardstock for your envelope to your cutting mat. If you are using the same cardstock as your card, keep your dial set to "light cardstock." If you choose something sturdier, adjust your dial to "Cardstock +." Cut your design.

Step 4

If you are using an acetate liner, send the envelope file to cut again, this time on your acetate paper. Adjust your dial to "cardboard." Trim the sides of the liner and slice off the bottom portion of the acetate liner. Use adhesive scrapbooking tape to attach the acetate to the inside of the envelope piece.

Step 5

Fold the envelope's edges up and use adhesive scrapbooking tape to secure the edges. Use your scoring tool to enhance the crease of the envelope flap, if you deem it necessary.

Luggage Tag Wedding Favor

What you'll need:
- Luggage tag holder, clear or lightly tinted to match your wedding colors
- Cardstock in the main color of your wedding
- Sticky foil in your secondary wedding color

Step 1

In Design Space, open the "Luggage Tag" template from the Design Space Library. Write out any wording or place any images on your workspace to be cut out of the sticky foil. Cut out the luggage tag on the cardstock.

Step 2

Print and cut the wording or images on your sticky foil. Weed out any parts of the cut that you do not want as part of your design.

Step 3

Transfer the wording to your cardstock luggage tag using your scoring tool to make sure it firmly attaches. Remove the backing materials when you are sure it is secure.

Step 4

Slide the cardstock luggage tag into the clear luggage tag holder and you now have a custom, handmade wedding favor to add to your welcome bag!

Custom Stickers and Labels

Project inspired by Damask Love

Kids love stickers. Grown up's love stickers. Let's face it, everyone loves stickers. Stickers and labels are so easy to make, and the options are endless for all your crafting and gifting needs. You can choose a single theme for the sticker sheet or add various designs that you love. You can also find pre-made sticker templates in the Design Space library or make your own from shapes and images.

You'll need:
- Sheets of sticker paper in various colors

Step 1
Open up Design Space and upload your sticker or label images or add your own images, words, and shapes that you want.

Make sure to remove the backgrounds of images that you do not want to have as part of the stickers. Make sure to see a checkered section where the background used to be to make sure it was removed.

Step 2
Keep adding and adjusting your images to cover the entire space of your sticker sheet.

Step 3
Load your sticker paper on your cutting mat and send your file to print and cut. When printing stickers, it is normal for the edges to look blurry. This process allows you to have a cut image that is full color.

Step 4
Peel your sticker paper from the mat and start sticking them around or add them to your next gift!

Holiday Welcome Mat

Project inspired by Everyday Jenny

Having a themed doormat or welcome mat is wonderful, but it can get expensive every time you want to switch it out for the holidays. But when you have a Cricut, the world is much more affordable! You can add text and images for anything you desire. Welcome guests in style and season from here on out.

You'll need:
- Plain doormat
- Black and green outdoor paint
- Paintbrushes
- Stencil vinyl
- Spray adhesive

Step 1
Open Design Space and create your message and images you want to have on your welcome mat. Make sure to scale them to fit your project size. When you have your design created, send the file to cut out of your stencil vinyl.

Step 2
Take your stencil from your mat and spray it with spray adhesive. Press the stencil down on your mat where you want the design to appear. Lay a piece of freezer paper over your stencil and place a few heavy books or weights over the stencil. Let it sit with this pressure for at least one hour to make sure the stencil is well attached.

Step 3
Begin painting your stencil when it is done attaching. Use a brush with stiff bristles and stipple it into the fibers of the mat. Try to get the color down deep into the mat. Rub the colors in on top to get a saturated top layer.

Step 4
Once you are done painting, gently peel away your stencil and let your mat dry in a place with good ventilation. The welcome mat must dry for at least 24 hours. Once it is done drying, place it on your front porch and welcome your guests with style!

Photograph Magnets

Project inspired by Cricut Design Space

Photo magnets are always sure to please and light up a fridge or magnetic board. An added benefit of this project is that it is incredibly easy to do! Make a bunch to place on your own fridge or give them out as gifts this year to family and friends.

You'll need:
- Magnetic sheets that can be cut and printed on by your Cricut
- Vinyl, if you prefer

Step 1

Open Design Space and upload the photograph you want to use. Adjust the image to fit the size and shape that you want to create. In this example, the photograph is surrounded by a frame and is a rectangle shape. You can also add images like stamps on top or have the photograph cut into shapes like hearts and stars.

Step 2

Send your file to print and cut and load your magnetic sheets onto your cutting mats. Peel the excess magnetic sheet away and you have yourself beautiful custom magnets!

Step 3

If you do not want to print directly onto the magnet, consider printing onto vinyl first then applying the vinyl to your magnetic sheets. Once your vinyl is attached to your magnet sheet, cut the file so it is cut in one step.

Floral Arrangement with Vellum Flowers

Project inspired by Create and Babble

Floral arrangements are gorgeous, but real flowers die and silk flowers collect amazing amounts of dust. But vellum flowers?

Those you can rinse and let air dry and they retain their beauty forever. You can create a variety of flowers and colors to decorate for a holiday or occasion.

You'll need:
- White and yellow vellum or yellow cardstock
- Floral tape
- Floral wire or straws
- Brads
- Hot glue

Step 1

In Design Space, create a new workspace and design your petal shapes. Lay out the project so you can create many flowers on your vellum. The petals of the flowers above are circles with a hole cut out of the middle and a slit going from one edge to the center.

Add a wavy pattern to the edges of the circles. For the center flower, if you are using vellum, create a long rectangle with multiple slits in the design. If you are using paper, you can slice them into rectangles, roll them into tubes and make cuts about three-quarters of a way down the tube. When you have your designs created, send the file to cut. Load your vellum and follow the prompts.

Step 2

Once your petals are cut, add a thin line of glue to one edge or the slit and press the other side on top to create the bowl shape.

Begin stacking a few of these petal shapes together. Slide a single brass brad through the hole and open the prongs to secure the petals together. Add a dab of glue to the top of the brad and press one yellow center into the center of the flower.

Step 3

Pull one side of the brass brad back to the center and slide it into a straw or attach it to floral wire with floral tape. You can also add a bit of glue to help reinforce the connection.

Step 4

Continue this process to make a bouquet of flowers and place them in a vase or other container to display. You can stick the straws or wire through the floral foam to keep them in a specific arrangement.

If you want this to be the permanent display, consider adding glue to the place where the stem inserts into the foam to keep it in place.

Step 5

If you used foam, make sure to place something over the top of the foam to cover it up. Shredded paper or filling is a great option for this design. Once you have it designed, place your new floral arrangement on the table or mantelpiece with pride!

Geometric Lampshade or Hanging Décor

Project inspired by I Like That Lamp

While this pendant may look intricate, it is actually an easy design that can add a little modernism to your space. You can use it as a lampshade, or you can add it to your décor for just a design detail. Also, you can consider adding a metallic version on the inside of the white pendant to add a little sparkle and interest to the project.

You'll need:
- White cardstock
- Metallic cardstock, if you prefer
- Ribbon or string
- Hot glue gun

Step 1
In Design Space, go into the library and enter the "Make It Now" section. Find the project labeled "Geo Ball."

Step 2
Once the project loads, place your cardstock on your cutting mat and send it to score the fold lines.

Step 3
Once your paper is scored, glue the metallic and white pieces of paper together. Begin folding the paper to create the geometric shape. Place a line of glue along one edge and bring the project into its final shape.

Step 4
If you are hanging your pendant, make sure to attach your ribbon or string to the bottom of the shape and hand it from your ceiling!

Takeout-style Boxes

Project inspired by Homemade Gifts Made Easy

If you are hosting a dinner party, you may want to send guests home with leftovers. Yes, you could use the go-to plastic to-go containers, or you could whip up a few custom ones of your own. You can serve leftovers in these simple packages or you can add all sorts of embellishments, like stickers and labels.

You'll need:
- Sticker paper for labels or stickers
- Cardstock
- Hot glue gun or glue dots

Step 1
If you are going to add labels of stickers to your boxes, design them in Design Space with the image or text that you prefer. Consider adding the title of the event and the date to the label so guests know right away how long they have the leftovers for in their fridge.

Create a variety of sizes so they will fit over the cardstock boxes you are about to create or other containers you might need to use.

Step 2

Once your stickers or labels are created, send the file to print and cut.

Step 3

Search in the Design Space library the template for Chinese Take Out Boxes and load it into a new workspace. Choose a variety of sizes. Load your cardstock onto your cutting mats and send the file to cut.

Step 4

Fold your cut cardstock along the score lines. Apply glue along the edges to assemble the box and reinforce the seams.

Step 5

If you are adding stickers to your boxes, add them now. For other containers, keep the stickers nearby or apply them onto them as well. You are ready to send your guests away in style now!

Latte Stencil

Project inspired by Repurposing Junkie

Up your morning coffee game with a dash of cinnamon or espresso powder over the foam. You can also adapt this to add a dash of cocoa over whipped cream on a hot chocolate.

You'll need:
- Cardstock or vellum
- Coffee in a mug and a dusting material

Step 1
Measure the top of your mugs or your favorite mug you use often. In Design Space, create a circle or shape that will rest over the lip of your mug and add another small circle to the side of it to be the tab that you will hold while the stencil is in use.

Step 2
Write your message or create your image on your stencil. Make sure to center your image in the shape. Send the file to cut on your vellum. Weed the small pieces in the center of your design and peel away the outside vellum or cardstock you do not need.

Step 3
When your latte is ready and still nice and hot, place the stencil over your mug and tap your dusting flavor over top of the stencil. Gently lift the stencil away to reveal your barista design. If you used vellum, wash the stencil off and lay aside to dry for your next coffee creation!

Felt Owls

Project inspired by Lia Griffith

You can use these as ornaments or hang around for some fun fall décor. You can also have your kids help you create these adorable pinecone owls.

You'll need:
- Various pinecones washed and air dried
- Felt in various colors like brown, black, white, yellow, and teal
- Hot glue gun
- Ribbon

Step 1
To begin, you will want to design the pieces of the owl face and wings in Design Space. The face is made of two large circles attached to one another. The eyes are two layered circles and the nose is a teardrop shape.

The wings are two layered teardrops and can have small circle embellishments. You can also create a stomach piece, which is a circle with small circles inside of it. "Eyebrows" in two wings or a small triangle are also good embellishments to design.

Step 2
Send your images to cut out of your felt. Tape down your felt pieces with masking tape or painter's tape if you want to make sure the fabric does not move around while cutting.

Step 3
Begin creating your pinecone owls by taking the pieces and start gluing them onto the pinecone. Alternate colors and styles to create a little village of owls. Glue a small piece of glue to the top of the pinecones to be able to hang them, if you want, or leave them to set flat on a surface.

Paper Flower Wreath

Project inspired by The Crafty Blog Stalker

Decorate your door with a festive wreath. You can make it any colors or styles you want based on your décor and taste. Make sure that when you are selecting your colors that you also choose a color "pop," like the teal color in this example.

Also, make sure to make different leaves out of green colors. Your wreath base can be anything like foam or twine. If you have a base that is not attractive, grab some coordinating fabric to wrap around the wreath or make enough flowers and leaves to completely cover the base. You can also add embellishments like beads, buttons, felt balls, and more to your project to take it up a notch.

You'll need:
- Wreath base
- Colored cardstock
- Hot glue gun
- Coordinated fabric, if desired

Step 1
In Design Space, find a variety of different flower and leaf projects. Aim for about three or four different flower designs that are different in size. Try to make as many as possible in different colors and sizes.

Follow the instructions for compiling the petals and creating the flowers. Pinch the leaves or fold the bottoms over to add dimension to the leaves. A good goal is to have about 30 different flowers and 15 different leaves to start.

Step 2
If you decided to wrap your wreath with fabric, add a little glue to one end of the fabric to the wreath and begin wrapping it around the wreath and securing the other end with hot glue when it is covered.

You do not need to cover the whole wreath with fabric or use it at all, just make enough flowers and leaves to cover any exposed wreath base that you do not want to be seen.

Step 3
Begin adding your flowers to your wreath with your hot glue gun. Make sure you are mixing shapes and colors on your wreath. Once all the flowers are added to your wreath, fill in with the leaves. Add other embellishments if you want. When the glue is dry, get ready to hang your wreath!

Felted Animal Masks

Project inspired by Lia Griffith

Choose your animal and adapt accordingly. You can make these for a dress-up box or Halloween costume. They are also great accessories for adult themed parties.

You'll need:

- Felt – various colors
- Fabric Glue
- Scissors
- Ribbon or string

Step 1

In Design Space, look through the library to find a mask template for the animal you want. There are typically plenty of options available, but you can also develop your own design if you want. Also, make sure to adjust the sizing of the mask to fit a child or an adult.

Step 2

Adjust your design to reflect the different colors of your mask. This will alert your machine to cut out the shapes from different colors of felt. Send the file to cut when you are ready.

Step 3

Use your fabric glue to attach all the pieces of the mark together. If you decide to use adhesive fabric instead of felt, use transfer tape to help attach all the pieces to one another. Also, the mask should have two holes punched in either side of the mask. If it does not, you will want to add a couple holes and then string your ribbon through to be able to tie it around your head.

If you want to add more design to it, consider adding embroidery, sequins, or glitter to your masks.

Troubleshooting

→ Optimizing speed and connection

Generally speaking, working with the Design Space software is pretty easy and free from glitches and problems. Of course, there is always room for improvement and errors that occur throughout the process, as is the case with anything technology-related, right? The most common complaints about the software system for Cricut is that it fails to open, freezes up, is slow to load, and crashes. To help you troubleshoot some of these common errors, follow the advice below.

The first thing you should check is your Internet connection. This is the primary cause of Design Space problems. You need a good upload and download speed consistently for the program to run smoothly.

Spikes and dips in your connection can make things glitch. If you can, try placing your router next to your machine so it can get a consistent connection.

Some websites and software only need a good download speed but does not depend on upload speed. This is not the case with Design Space. You need both for it to work well. This is because you are constantly uploading information and downloading information into the system for your various projects. Having a good download speed is great, but if your upload speed is slow, you could experience some slow loading, etc.

To learn about your computer Internet speed, try running a test. There are various services out there like Ookla or speedtest.net that will help you learn more about your Internet speed. In order to properly test this, you will want to have a Bluetooth connection or a USB port open. Remember, the speeds you need, according to Cricut, are 1 or 2 Mbps for uploading and 2 or 3 Mbps for downloading. If you run a test and your numbers are lower than this, call up your Internet provider and ask for a new modem or router. It can be a pain waiting for it to arrive, but it can make a huge difference if your current one is just not cutting it.

Sometimes it is not a problem with your Internet. Sometimes it is a problem with your computer or the device you are trying to work in Design Space from. Like your Internet speeds, Cricut has guidelines for optimal operations. Below is a breakdown of the primary requirements for different types of computers:

Apple Computers:
- 1.83 GHz CPU
- 4GB Ram
- 50MB free space
- Bluetooth enabled or available USB port
- MAC OS X 10.12 or newer operating system

Windows Computers
- 4GB Ram
- 50MB free space
- Bluetooth enabled or open USB port
- AMD processor or Intel Core series
- Windows 8 or newer operating system

Sometimes all you need to do is clear up some space on your computer or update your operating system (happens automatically) to optimize Design Space on your device. Other times it is not really about the space or operating system on your computer, but it has to do with the other programs running in the background at the same time as Design Space.

Anything that you have open while you are trying to use Design Space can cause a drain on the program. This is especially true if the other program is using your Internet to download or upload or stream information from the Internet. You may not need to close down all your open programs aside from Design Space, but try shutting a couple down that you think could be slowing you down.

In addition to the above general troubleshooting suggestions, here are a few more suggestions to help your general problems:

- Check malware and clean up as necessary
- Defrag your hard drive
- For Windows users, update your drivers
- Update antivirus software if necessary
- Clear out your history and cache (with ccleaner)

These can help your Internet speed but can also potentially solve your problems. Browser choice is another option to check out. It is important that you are using the newest version of the browser for the best results. Make sure it is up to date, no matter if you are using Edge, Firefox, Mozilla, Safari, or Chrome. This update can make a world of difference.

And, of course, if all else fails, contact Cricut customer service! They are trained and knowledgeable at dealing with a host of problems. If you have a more specific problem, try browsing the solutions provided below before giving them a call, though. You just might surprise yourself how technologically-savvy you are at fixing the problem on your own!

→ Calibration of "Print then Cut" is Not Working Properly

"Print then Cut" is a great feature you should consider exploring with your Cricut Explore. Basically, this function means that you print an image on your regular printer and then can put it in your Cricut Explore to cut around the edges. The first time you go to use this function, it is going to ask you to calibrate, but some people can face the frustrating situation when the machine does not read the sensor marks. Those with a Cricut One or Cricut Air also have this function, but their machines come pre-calibrated, so this is usually not a problem for these machines.

The calibration process for the Cricut Explore includes:

1. Open Design Space and click on "Print then Cut" image, and then select "Go."
2. On your first time with this feature, the software will prompt you to print a page for calibration. This page should print on your regular printer.
3. When you have finished printing, place the page on a cutting mat and load it into your Cricut Explore. Press the "Go" button to tell the machine to cut.
4. Ideally, your machine will read the sensor marks on the calibration page and make a few test cuts and then prompt you with questions about the cuts.
5. A few more testing cuts will be made after you answer the first round of questions. After this second round of cuts, you will be asked more questions.

6. Once you finish answering all the questions, your machine will be calibrated for "Print then Cut."

For some, this process shuts down and does not complete the cut marks, meaning it cannot make it through the calibration process. There are many reasons for this, but here are a few to troubleshoot to see if one of these issues is causing it:

1. Check that your printed calibration page has all the sensor marks showing and are complete. Sometimes the file from Design Space does not get read properly by your printer and it can trim the sensor marks off. If this happens to you, go to the website for Cricut and download the calibration page from there. Print that one and make sure the sensor marks are correct. This is usually the best fix for this problem.

2. Adjust the lighting in your room. Sometimes a very brightly lit room can cause a misreading of the sensor marks. Adjust your lighting so it is softer and try again.

3. Clean off your cutting mat. A dirty mat can cause a misreading of your calibration page or it does not stay in place when cutting. Try cleaning it off and trying it again, or use a different cutting mat if you have one.

4. Check the alignment of your calibration page on your cutting mat. Make sure you placed it in the correct spot for the process. Adjust as necessary and try cutting again.

If none of these solutions fix your problem, try contacting Cricut for more assistance. There may be something else wrong with your machine or materials.

→ **The incorrect cartridge name appears on the Cricut screen**

Follow the following steps to correct the error:

1. Sometimes in manufacturing, the cartridge stickers are placed on backward on the cartridge. Take out the inserted cartridge and reinsert it backward to check if this is the problem. If this does not solve the problem, move to the next step.
2. Does this happen with all cartridges?
   a) Yes - Move to the next step
   b) No - Call customer service or chat online with customer service if it still displays the wrong name after putting it in backward.
3. Hard reset may be required at this point. Follow the directions in the user manual for this. Again, if this does not fix the problem, move to the next step.
4. Update Firmware, especially if it is not up to date. If this does not fix the problem, move to the next step.
5. Call customer service or chat online with customer service if none of the above steps solved the problem.

→ **When images are added to the queue, the Cricut machine freezes**

Before selecting the image keys, always select the gray feature keys.

Follow the following steps to correct the error if it is still occurring:

1. Turn off the Cricut and let it rest for up to one hour. Let it rest for at least a minimum of 10 minutes.

2. Double check how the characters were entered. Try re-entering the characters in the accurate order allowing the image to show up on the screen before keying in the subsequent character.
3. "Characters won't fit" appears when the image memory is exceeded in the queue. Try removing images to see if the problem is fixed. If the problem continues, proceed to the next step.
4. If you insert another cartridge, does this error still occur?
   a) YES - Move to the next step.
   b) NO - Call customer service or chat online customer service to speak with them about the error.
5. Hard reset may be required at this point. Follow the directions in the user manual for this. Again, if this does not fix the problem move to the next step.
6. Update Firmware, especially if it is not up to date. If this does not fix the problem, move to the next step.
7. Call customer service or chat online with customer service if none of the above steps solved the problem.

→ **The Cricut Machine keypad has glitches**

There are two common keyboard errors that occur: the buttons do not respond when pressed and none of the buttons will work despite lights being lit on the keyboard. If this does not explain your problem, call customer service or chat online with customer service about the problem. If your error is one of the two most common problems, follow the steps below for whichever your problem is.

Non-responsive buttons when pressed:

1. Check that the machine recognizes the inserted cartridge by making sure the screen displays the cartridges name. If this does not fix the problem, move to the next step.
2. Check that the mat is loaded into the machine properly. If this does not fix the problem, move to the next step.
3. If you insert another cartridge, does this error still occur?
   a) YES - Move to the next step.
   b) NO - Call customer service or chat online customer service to speak with them about the error.
4. Hard reset may be required at this point. Follow the directions in the user manual for this. Again, if this does not fix the problem move to the next step.
5. Update Firmware, especially if it is not up to date. If this does not fix the problem, move to the next step.
6. Call customer service or chat online with customer service if none of the above steps solved the problem.

No buttons will respond despite lights coming on:

1. Update Firmware, especially if it is not up to date. Lights on the left side of the keyboard, the power button, and the cut button will light up when in Firmware mode. If this does not fix the problem, move to the next step.
2. Call customer service or chat online with customer service if the above step did not solve the problem.

→ **Unloading or loading the mat makes the Cricut machine freeze**

Follow the following steps to correct the error:

1. Turn off the Cricut and let it rest for up to one hour. Let it rest for at least a minimum of 10 minutes.
2. Did you switch a cartridge while the machine was on? This is called "hot swapping" and can result in the machine freezing.
3. YES - Turn off your machine and switch the cartridge. If this does not solve the problem, move to the next step.
4. NO - Move to the next step.
5. If you insert another cartridge, does this error still occur?
   a) YES - Move to the next step.
   b) NO - Call customer service or chat online customer service to speak with them about the error.
6. Hard reset may be required at this point. Follow the directions in the user manual for this. Again, if this does not fix the problem move to the next step.
7. Update Firmware, especially if it is not up to date. If this does not fix the problem, move to the next step.
8. Call customer service or chat online with customer service if none of the above steps solved the problem.

→ **During cutting, the carriage does not travel along the track**

Follow the following steps to correct the error:

1. Can the carriage car move easily to the right and left while the machine is on?
   a) YES - Move to the next step.

b) NO - Call customer service or chat online customer service to speak with them about the problem.

2. Look carefully at the belt, roller bars, and carriage car to see if any damage is evident. Take photos of any observed damage and Call customer service or chat online customer service to speak with them about the problem.

a) Belt - Is it lose or broken?

b) Carriage car - Is it on the track? Is it on the track straight?

3. Call customer service or chat online customer service to speak with them about the problem if no damage is obvious.

→ **When loaded into the Cricut machine, the mat becomes crooked**

Do not hold the corners or sides of the mat when loading it. Instead, hold the bottom in the center and position the mat slightly under and against the roller bar's rubber rings. This is easiest when the bottom of the mat is lifted gently.

Follow the following steps to correct the error:

1. Look carefully at the roller bar to see if any damage is evident. Take photos of any observed damage and Call customer service or chat online customer service to speak with them about the problem. If there is no damage noticeable, move on to the next step.

2. The correct mat size must be used for the machine. Double check it is correct. If this does not fix the problem, move on to the next step.

3. Before loading the mat, make sure it is aligned with guides, and the mat's edges are below the roller bar. If this does not fix the problem, move on to the next step.

4. As the roller bar begins to roll, lightly press the mat underneath with gentle pressure.

5. Call customer service or chat online with customer service if none of the above steps solved the problem.

→ During cutting, the machine freezes

Follow the following steps to correct the error:

1. Turn off the Cricut and let it rest for up to one hour. Let it rest for at least a minimum of 10 minutes.
2. If you insert another cartridge, does this error still occur?
   a) YES - Move to the next step.
   b) NO - Call customer service or chat online customer service to speak with them about the error.
3. Hard reset may be required at this point. Follow the directions in the user manual for this. Again, if this does not fix the problem, move to the next step.
4. Update Firmware, especially if it is not up to date. If this does not fix the problem, move to the next step.
5. Call customer service or chat online with customer service if none of the above steps solved the problem

→ Red Banner Error Messages in Design Space

Occasionally, you will encounter an error message in Design Space that you cannot resolve with any of the tips above. When this happens, and you see one of the following messages, work through the suggestions here according to the device you are working on.

Typical error messages include:
- "Project Not Loading"
- "Custom Materials Warning"
- "Project Retrieval Error"
- "Unable to Load Pen Colors"

Other times, you will receive many errors at once. All of these warrant a different approach and perspective to your troubleshooting process.

To begin, consider closing down the software program and re-launch. This means "exit" or "quit." This is also a good time to clear your Internet's cookies and cache if you have not already. If this simple approach does not fix your error messages, you may want to clear your "DNS" cache. To clear this, you will need to approach it in a different way according to your operating system.

For Windows users:
1. Open your Start menu.
2. Open or choose Command Prompt, sometimes requiring you to right-click to open properly.
   a. Windows 7 & 8: enter "cmd" in the search bar and select "Command Prompt." Then select "Run as Administrator."
   b. Windows 10: Right-click the Start menu and select "Command Prompt (Admin)"
3. Enter "ipconfig/flushdns"
4. The system is now going to run the process and let you know when it is done.
5. When done, type in "exit"

Now go back to Design Space and try again to see if your errors are resolved.

In general, one of the best places to find help troubleshooting a problem or error is on the Cricut website or by calling a representative. There are a host of suggestions online that you could try in addition to these, such as reconfiguring your ISP server to a Google Public DNS server, but those types of fixes are best left to IT professionals. Most likely, you can resolve any issue from the basic troubleshooting in here or found on the website. **https://help.cricut.com/hc/en-us**

Tips, Tools and Techniques

When you are working on your projects, you may come across some things that you wish were easier or would help you move from one design to the next more seamlessly. Yes, you can get a host of tips on the Cricut website, however, throughout this chapter, you will discover some not-so-common tips as well.

Tips for Success - Every Time

1. If you have stubborn materials gripping your mat when you are done with a project, use a lint roller to help get these pieces off. To clean it more, use a little soap and a clean cloth to wash it. Make sure to rinse the mat with clean water and allow it to air dry.

2. If you are working with paper, prevent the edges from curling by removing the mat, not removing the paper from the mat.

3. Try different brands of pens with your projects and in your machines.

4. Before you are ready to cut on your final materials, try it out on scrap materials first. This way, you can make sure it is as you planned and can make any changes you need.

5. If you want to use a personal image, make sure to save it to your computer as a SCG, JPEG, or PNG.

6. You can download free fonts from sites like 1001freefonts.com, fontsquirrel.com, and dafont.com that can be used in Cricut.

7. If you are stuck without the preferred color of vinyl, consider using spray paint to color it in a pinch.

8. Become familiar with how to use different materials with your machine by reading up on it at Cricut.com.

9. Have a blade designated for each medium you cut. For example, label blades for paper, vinyl, wood, metal, etc. This helps blades have a longer lifespan and better quality cut.

10. If you want to design a customized stencil, cut it out of freezer paper. It is one of the best mediums to use for this.

Cricut and Cutting Tips

If you have a material that is not sticking well to your mat, add a little bit of painter's tape or electrical tape to the edges. If you need to make a thick cut, it may not always happen on the first pass. Do not take your project off the mat and try cutting by hand. Instead, tell the machine to cut again by selecting "Go" or "C."

Tips on how to Print and Cut

If you have one or can purchase one, an ink jet printer is your best option for printers and the Cricut. Laser printers often heat ink too hot for the Cricut to read properly.

For finding large images, use Safari or Internet Explorer. Firefox and Chrome have smaller images because of browser capabilities.

To get the best registration of a print, use white paper. If the project calls for colored paper, print the images and marks on white first and tape it over the colored paper to be cut in your Cricut.

Cricut and Writing Tips
Keep your pens in a container with the tip facing down. This keeps ink in the tip of the pen for best writing.

Thicken your pen's tip with a little bit of painter's tape or electrical tape wrapped around the tip.

Cricut and Scoring Tips
Stick your scoring tool in the spot for pens and you will have a nice folded piece of paper every time. If you want a very deep scoreline, add two or three scorelines to your project.

Cricut Embossing
Yes, you can emboss! Instead of loading a blade into the adapter, place your scoring stylus instead. Send a file you want embossed to "cut" but the stylus will actually emboss instead.

Cricut Blade Tips
When you have used your blades for a bit, you will want to sharpen them for the best results. Send a very basic design to be cut and lay a sheet of aluminum foil on the cutting mat. This will sharpen it back quickly.

Cricut Designing Tips
Choose your Internet wisely. Google Chrome does not usually work well with Design Space. Consider using Safari or Firefox instead.

Often Design Space will offer different images or projects for free as a limited promotion. To help you take advantage of the free items and store them easily, open a new canvas and upload the project. Save the project with a description of it as the name of the project.

When you want to cut the design you created exactly how it is laid out, make sure to select "All" and then "Attach." This is what lets you keep everything in place without the machine thinking it needs to do multiple cuts.

Handbooks are great instructional resources. When you are starting to learn how to use cartridges, use this link: www.home.cricut.com/handbooks

When you are making an intricate design with many layers, put the small and intricate pieces on the bottom layers and the larger ones on the top in Design Space. This means when the file is cut, the largest layer is cut last so that the vinyl does not risk being moved around during the smaller cuts.

Cricut Mat Tips
If your cutting mats are beginning to lose stickiness, use disinfecting wipes to help bring it back. If a cut goes through your mat, place a piece or two of duct tape underneath to give you more longevity from the mat.

Do not use the same side or end of the mat all the time. Make sure to rotate it to get the longest lifespan of it. Definitely do this if you are making the same design over and over again.

To save money or get more wear out of a mat, consider cutting a 12" x 24" mat in half to make two 12" x 12" mats.

Materials

Purchasing materials online is often the most cost-effective strategy. In addition, you can typically get scraps of vinyl from local sign shops in your area.

If you cannot find a certain color of cardstock, consider printing it instead onto white cardstock.

Store toilet paper rolls or paper towel rolls to keep bundles of unused vinyl in.

In the event you do not have transfer paper, clear contact paper can work wonders in removing the backing of your vinyl and iron-on.

Weeding Tips

If you do not have a weeding tool, grab a safety pin instead and use the pointed end to get out those stubborn little pieces that you do not want. Also, wear a headlamp to help you see what you are working on. If all else fails, consider sitting by a bright window. You can invest in something a bit more high-tech to help with weeding if you want. The Cricut BrightPad is a great tool to invest in. It offers a LED lightbox for you to use in weeding.

Project Assembly Suggestions

Self-adhesive foam mounting pieces and glue dots are your best friends. Even adhesive cardboard pieces are great to always keep on hand. This can add depth to just about any project and bring it from average to outstanding immediately.

Another good assembly tool to have on hand is a glue that is super sticky and dries fast. You should also choose a glue that is designed for the material you are working on, like metal, wood, or glass. Sometimes you may want to use a tacky glue so that you can move the items around a bit after you placed them.

Materials to Get Your Creative Mind Reeling

Below is a not-completely-comprehensive list of different materials you can experiment with using your Cricut. Some may sound totally out of the ordinary, while others have appeared in the various projects throughout this book. The idea of this list is to help get your creative "juices" flowing and to encourage you to try out different projects to see how it goes!

On a side note, if a material is thinner than 2 mm, a Cricut Explore can cut it. If you have a Cricut Maker, you can cut any material as long as it is thinner than 2.4 mm! Happy cutting!

Papers
- Kraft boards
- Glitter paper
- Glitter cardstock
- Freezer paper
- Foil embossed paper
- Foil poster boards
- Flocked paper
- Flocked cardstock
- Smooth cardboard
- Copy paper
- Construction paper
- Cereal boxes

- Regular cardstock
- Adhesive cardstock
- White core cardstock
- Wax paper
- Watercolor paper
- Solid core cardstock
- Shimmer paper
- Scrapbooking paper
- Rice paper
- Poster boards
- Post-its
- Photo framing, matting material
- Photographs
- Pearl paper
- Pearl cardstock
- Paper boards
- Parchment paper
- Paper grocery bags
- Notebook paper
- Metallic poster boards
- Metallic paper
- Metallic cardstock
- Kraft paper

Vinyl Materials
- Outdoor
- Metallic
- Matte
- Holographic
- Glossy
- Glitter
- Dry erase
- Chalkboard
- Adhesive

- Printable
- Stencil

Iron-on Transfer
- Printable
- Neon
- Metallic
- Matte
- Holographic
- Glossy
- Glitter
- Foil
- Flocked

Textiles or Fabrics

When cutting on fabric, add iron-on interfacing or stabilizer before placing it on your mat. This will help make sure your materials do not pull in the cutting process. Brands for interfacing include Heat n'Bond and Wonder Under. You can find them in craft stores or in the fabric section at Walmart.

- Polyester
- Oilcloth
- Metallic leather
- Linen
- Leather
- Flannel
- Felt
- Faux suede
- Faux leather
- Duck cloth
- Denim
- Cotton

- Canvas
- Burlap
- Printable fabrics
- Wool felt
- Silk

Additional Materials to Consider
- Magnetic sheets
- Glitter Foam
- Foil acetate
- Embossable foil
- Duct tape
- Craft foam
- Corrugated paper
- Cork boards
- Birchwood
- Balsa wood
- Aluminum foil
- Aluminum sheets
- Adhesive wood
- Adhesive foil
- Window Clings
- Washi tape
- Washi sheets
- Vellum
- Transparency film
- Temporary tattoo papers
- Tissue paper
- Stencil materials
- Soda Cans
- Shrink plastic
- Printable sticker paper
- Printable magnet sheets
- Plastic packaging

- Paint chips
- Metallic vellum
- Wrapping paper
- Wood veneer

Working with a Cricut Maker

If you have the joy of owning a Cricut Maker, you can cut even more projects than with other Cricut machines. This means you have even more crafting potential! The machine cuts with ten times more force and also offers a knife or rotary blade for your projects. The additional materials you can cut with your Cricut Maker include:

- Velvet
- Tweed
- Tulle
- Terry cloth
- Muslin
- Seersucker
- Knits
- Jute
- Jersey
- Fleece
- Cashmere
- Chiffon

Additional Tools

Of course, you have probably heard and learned by now how important it is to have the Cricut tools for your projects, but there are a few other crafting materials and tools that can help you expand your creativity and project potential. Below are some suggestions to get your mind spinning:

1. Dremel Moto-Saw: Attach this handy little cutter to the side of any table or counter and offers you the scroll saw ability for woodworking projects.

2. Willow Charcoal: This is a great marking tool that is easily covered with paint, unlike traditional pencils and markers. It also easily erases and has a fun, artistic appearance to the lines.

3. Chalkboard paints and chalkboard paint pens: So many projects can be turned into chalkboard surfaces, especially if your original plan did not turn out as you envisioned. A quick few coats of chalkboard paint on anything from an old vase to a wall space can turn a disaster into a fun, motivational message.

4. A set of tools for cutting linoleum: This may sound odd, but these little tools are awesome for cutting weird surface or engraving in leather. You can use them to make custom stamps or even carve weird surfaces (like pumpkins!)

5. Dremel rotary tool kit: This multi-functional tool is excellent for any action like buffing, drilling, and sanding. You can use this to smooth edges of materials (think the edges of the metal coasters in the etching chapter!) or carve a piece of stone (excellent canvas for vinyl or stenciling!)

6. A good quality drill: This is a bit of an investment, but if you are serious about your DIY projects, there is nothing better to have on hand than one of these. There really is nothing you cannot do with a drill!

7. A good glue gun: You will use this tool over and over again. Getting a gun that is a high-temperature is ideal,

but remember to watch your fingers! Using a good glue gun, you can do things like cabochons, headbands, mini sculptures, and even stencils.

8. Serger: Any project that involves fabric can benefit from a serger. In addition, they are relatively easy to use, so it opens up a whole new level of crafts! This machine is different than a normal sewing machine. This type of machine is an overlock and finishes the edges of the fabric so they do not fray. Also, while you are sewing, the machine simultaneously trims your seam allowance for you. This means you cannot just sew with it, but finish your seams and trim all in one swoop. This can get pricey, so make sure to pick one in your budget that has a good reputation and a good warranty.

9. Xyron 1.5" sticker maker: As mentioned in the wooden earring project, this machine is handy for all sorts of projects including adding permanent adhesive to wooden pieces fast and easy. Anything thinner than a nickel and 1.5" or thinner can go through the machine and get edge-to-edge permanent adhesive added to it. It is great for adding sparkles to projects, too!

10. Exacto or crafting knife, plus extra blades: While the Cricut is your main cutting machine, there will be times when you want to make some small cuts on your own. This is your go-to tool for all things hand-cutting. Make sure to pick up those extra blades to have on hand because when the blade gets dull or chipped, your cutting precision goes down (and your frustration level goes up!). Thankfully, swapping out the blades is easy. Just try not to cut yourself! These knives are sharp. Sometimes wearing protective gloves is a good idea, especially if you are cutting something with your hand or fingers nearby.

11. Laminator: Yes, your Cricut can do amazing things. And it can create the appearance of a laminated project. But do you really want all that hassle, or do you just want to stick it in one end and have it come out the other ready to be trimmed? Laminators make life look so polished, it is hard to justify not having one as a "serious" crafter. If you have never considered one before, try out one and see the difference in your crafting. You will most likely be pleasantly surprised!

There are definitely more tools and tips than this, but hopefully, these shortlists can start to get your wheels turning and a shopping list form so that you can enjoy your creativity and Cricut for many projects to come. If your budget allows, stock up on all the things listed at once and then work your way through them for projects and crafts. Figure out which ones work best for you and what you are drawn to. If budget is a concern, consider the last few projects you chose to work on.

Think about what tool or material listed above would have made that project easier for you. Now, the next time you are picking up your crafting supplies, think about adding that to your shopping cart. If there is a project in this book that screams out to you, "Make me! I'm awesome!" then look for the materials and tools that would support that project and get to it!

Your personality and preferences will be what determines the best things for your projects. If you never want to work with wood or metal, a sanding dremel may not be the best tool for you. The same goes for the Serger. If you never plan on working with fabric, do not spend your money on a pricey machine that will sit in your storage.

The bottom line: before you get super excited and let your creative mind run wild with your credit card, take a moment to think about what you would really want to make and would probably use, and start with those. You and your bank account will probably be much happier.

Conclusion

You have made it to the end of this book!

Let's hope it was informative and provided you with enough inspiration for all your future DIY and crafting dreams.

The next step is to pick out a project, gather the supplies, and get going! There are so many great ideas, many of which can be adjusted to your needs so it may take a bit to narrow down your first project.

It is normal to feel overwhelmed with ideas, so much so that it is almost paralyzing. If it helps, try choosing a chapter to start with. Maybe you choose one that you are most familiar with, like paper projects, or have always wanted to try out, like metal etching. From there, go through the chapter and choose a couple projects that interest you or that you think would fit for a need in your life, like a gift for an upcoming birthday or decoration for the next holiday.

When you have two or three projects in mind, look at your current crafting supplies. Do you have the majority of materials for one of those projects? If so, start with that one! If not, put all three projects in a hat and draw one. If you like it, do it. If you feel a pang of sadness because you drew the name of a project you really did not want, then do the one you discovered you want to do!

The Cricut machine is user-friendly and versatile. There is hardly a limit to what you can do with your machine, and the projects can be fun and as challenging as you want to make them.

If you find a project that you truly enjoy and want to do over and over, go for it! If you keep playing around with new projects every time, that is amazing! The Cricut and even the tools suggested in the last chapter of this book are designed to encourage your creativity and make your experience of DIY easier. At this point, you need to stop reading and get making! Bust out the cardstock, vinyl, or leather.

Open up Design Space and get that machine working. And always take a moment when your project is all done to sit back and revel in the glory of your creation! You did it!

Finally, if you have comments (positive or negative), please let me know trough email at: contact@truecrafting.com

Thank you!

Resources

Throughout this book I have used inspiration from several cricut crafting blogs. I would like to share my go-to blogs to get inspiration for future projects.

Here are blogs I like to follow (in no particular order):

- joann.com/projects
- bespoke-bride.com
- inspirationmadesimple.com
- craftingintherain.com/category/cricut
- going-buggy.blogspot.com
- 100directions.com/tag/cricut
- alittlecraftinyourday.com
- papermilldirect.co.uk/inspire
- thisheartofmineblog.com
- inspiration.cricut.com
- lauraslittleparty.com
- mysparkledlife.com
- kimdellow.com
- thehappyscraps.com/category/diy-projects/cricut
- jennifermaker.com/cricut-maker-projects
- craftingafamily.com
- thesoutherncouture.com
- thesimplycraftedlife.com/category/cricut-projects
- heyletsmakestuff.com
- creativebug.com/cricut
- sewbon.com/tag/cricut
- attagirlsays.com/tag/cricut
- ithappensinablink.com/cricut-class-tutorials-and-projects
- printablecrush.com
- everydayjenny.com/cricut

- cherishedbliss.com
- carolescricutcrafts.com
- threelittlemonkeysstudio.com
- albiongould.com/tag/cricut
- hellocreativefamily.com
- iammommahearmeroar.net
- cmongetcrafty.com/tag/cricut
- lydioutloud.com
- damasklove.com/tag/cricut
- createandbabble.com/category/cricut
- homemade-gifts-made-easy.com
- repurposingjunkie.com/category/projects
- liagriffith.com
- thecraftyblogstalker.com/crafts
- liagriffith.com

Notes

Write down your settings, operating procedures, or something you would like to keep remembering when doing a certain project.

....

....

....

....

....

....

....

....

....

....

....

....

....

....

Printed in Great Britain
by Amazon